Ten Tips to Tame Your Teen

Strategies That Work!

By
Ray Erickson, LCSW

Bribing Didn't Work!
Grounding Didn't Work!
Yelling Didn't Work!
The Ten Tips Do Work!

Ten Tips
to
Tame Your
Teen
Strategies That Work!

By
Ray Erickson, LCSW
Licensed Clinical Social Worker

Illustrations by Bob Armstrong
Photography by Charlie Sussman

Imagination Beyond Limits
Sacramento, CA
916-333-4169
www.rayerickson.com
ray@rayerickson.com

Designed by Ray Erickson

Illustrations by Bob Armstrong

Photography by Charlie Sussman

Library of Congress Cataloging-in-Publication Data

Registration Number: TX 7-496-409

Erickson, Raymond E.
         Ten Tips to Tame Your Teen: Strategies that Work! / Ray Erickson

ISBN-13: 978-1456488734
         1. Parenting. 2. Teenagers. 3. Family Relationships. 1. Title

Contents

Ten Tips to Tame Your Teen

Introduction

or

Why This Book Will Help You.

I am so happy you have this book in your hands. I wrote it to give you some practical advice and effective ways to respond to what may or may not be *normal* adolescent behavior. I also wrote *Ten Tips to Tame Your Teen* to help you understand the nature of the beast, adolescence. I know you want to be more effective with your teen and in order to do that; you must know what you are dealing with. Adolescents are not young adults although I may use that term frequently in this book. They are not children either, even though I use that term frequently as well.

Adolescence is its own unique time of life. As much as your teenager wants to be treated like an adult; in your eyes they are still the children that you nurtured and raised with some blood, lots of sweat and the occasional tear. Because of this many parents believe that once their kids reach a certain age whether it is 12, 15 or 18 then somehow, they magically ripen into an ultra-responsible person, someone who has all of the skills needed to succeed in the world. I don't know where this magical thinking comes from but after working with families for more than 30 years I am amazed how many parents take a *close your eyes and cross your fingers* approach to preparing their kids for life.

In this book I propose a radical shift in thinking about teenagers. If there is one thing I want you to take away from reading this book it is a belief that your adolescent children are <u>already</u> capable and competent to the degree that you believe they are. Notice I said *to the degree that you <u>believe</u> they are capable and competent.*" Belief is a cornerstone of my work with parents and teenagers. The families I work with respond positively because they are able to shift their perspective from the more common belief that teenagers are incompetent and incapable to recognizing that their kids are <u>already</u> capable and competent but lack the experience and skills necessary to succeed in life. I am defining success as the degree of happiness one experiences in life.

The most important thing you can do is to believe in your kids and know they are competent and capable, right now. Ignore any physical evidence to the contrary and do this one thing. Soon, you will start to notice your teen behaving in ways that demonstrate competency. Try it, just start looking for the things they do well and you will begin to see them. Many parents believe their kids are good for nothing, lazy or otherwise hopeless. Guess what those parents see their teens doing? That's right their kids are fully cooperating with them by being good for nothing, lazy and otherwise hopeless.

Belief is extremely powerful and if I had a nickel for every time I said to a parent, *"You get what you expect,"* I would be a rich man.

What I am saying to you is this, when you believe your teenager is out of control, they will be out of control. When you believe your adolescent is not capable, then they will not be capable. When you believe your teen is not competent then they will be incompetent. You get what you believe them to be. Change this belief and you will change your life and theirs.

You have now taken the first step towards boldly going where no parents have gone before. Integrate The Ten Tips into your relationships and you not only enrich your life, but you will enrich the lives of those you love.

To get the most from this book, I recommend your read it three times. The first time you read the book, read it from cover to cover for general understanding of the principles. The second time you read it, highlight all of the parts that are important to you. The third time you read the book, focus only on the highlighted parts. This process helps you become very familiar with each of the Ten Tips as well as the overall message of this book. Do this and you will get off to a good start and you will supersize all ten tips.

Ten Tips to Tame Your Teen

Acknowledgments

I want to thank each and every teenager and parent who has crossed my path. If it were not for you this book could not have been written. I celebrate all of you.

I am also grateful to have by my side, my beautiful, intelligent and talented wife, Mercedes Alvarado and her undying support. Her presence in my life is nothing short of a miracle.

Thanks to my illustrator, Bob Armstrong who many years ago created the archetypal family that graces the pages of this book. I love his work.

My heartfelt thanks and appreciation go out to my best friend, and fellow social worker, Charlie Sussman, who lovingly provided the photography.

I want to thank all of the professionals I have worked with over the years, I learned so much from you.

Thanks also to all of you, who picked up this book and are reading it right now. You are the reason that I wrote it.

Ten Tips to Tame Your Teen

Ten Tips to Tame Your Teen

Strategies That Work!

Ten Tips to Tame Your Teen

Chapter 1
Brain Damaged

"When I was a boy of fourteen, my father was so ignorant I could hardly stand to have the old man around. But when I got to be twenty-one, I was astonished at how much he had learned in seven years." ~Mark Twain

You may not want to believe this, but when children become adolescents, <u>all</u> parents become *Brain Damaged*. It's true!! Adults, who were previously revered by their children, now have the brain capacity of a newt.

This viewpoint is shared by most adolescents, so why not use it to *your* advantage?

Surrender and declare yourself ignorant. Admit to yourself <u>and</u> your teen that you have <u>no</u> idea what their life is like, then the door to understanding opens.

If you are *Brain Damaged* enough, your teen will have mercy and explain their world to you with amazing detail. It helps to say things like,

> *"You're right; I don't have a clue, so give me a break."*

When you allow yourself to ***not*** know all of the answers, you reap the benefits of being *Brain Damaged*. This does not mean you are not the lord and master of your household. You are, but according your teen; you are feeble-minded and ignorant. Don't worry about it. It's no big deal. *Brain Damaged* is a powerful tool when you learn how to use it. Besides, when you are *Brain Damaged* your teen gets a chance to use their expanding brain capacity.

The first thing that changes with adolescence is their perception of you. It's important to know that this new perspective is biological and <u>not</u> an attitude problem. If your teen thinks you are *Brain Damaged,* it is not about you. When you understand that it is nature and not nurture then your ego will not feel threatened.

Brain Damaged suggests that you accept your adolescent's point of view as being true for them. It also helps to admit that you know nothing about their lives, or about anything else for that matter. As their brain gets bigger, your brain *appears* to get smaller. Of course your brain doesn't shrink but if you have forgotten what it's like to be a teenager then you will be confused about what your teenager needs. So keep this in mind; it is *because* of this shift in consciousness that teenagers are able to let go of their dependency upon you. Isn't that what you want? Isn't that what they need?

It doesn't matter how many degrees you have, or how important your job is. According to your teenager, you are clueless and ignorant. Get used to it. The good news is this is temporary. When adolescents have a sense of themselves as distinct and autonomous people, and they have been on their own for a while, they will once again recognize, appreciate and seek out your brilliance and wisdom. In the meantime, be grateful for the lessons your teen is teaching you as they transform themselves into the person they are truly meant to be.

Fun Facts about Adolescents

In his article, "Brain Development in Young Adolescents: Good News for Middle School Teachers," Peter Lorain, a retired high school teacher and middle school principal from Beaverton, Oregon says: "Although most people believe that cognitive development plateaus in early adolescence, current research shows that young adolescents go through tremendous brain growth and development. Far from being 'over the hill,' they are just beginning to encounter the mountain."

Brain Damage and Communication

A funny thing happens when you become *Brain Damaged*. Your teenager starts talking to you again. Really! They begin to tell you what their world is like. They tell you what's going on at school and what's going on with their friends. They also talk about their struggles, concerns, triumphs and tribulations.

It is essential that parents and other loving adults be open to the views and opinions of teenagers. These young people have fresh and innovative ideas which will become the foundation for their future, for your future and for society's future. There is too much at stake when it comes to adolescent development. Our lives depend upon their ability to come up with viable solutions to problems. The future of the world is literally in their hands. Yeah, it's scary, but it's true nonetheless. The relationship you build with your children is the vehicle that permits them to grow and mature. When you are open to your children's world view it supports their self-esteem and self-image. When you accept your teen's point of view as valid it inspires them to be confident, curious, and adventurous.

When you or other adults are closed to the views and ideas of teenagers, you sacrifice the chance to learn more about these amazing young men and women. When parents, teachers, and other well-meaning adults deny being *Brain Damaged,* they are deluding themselves. One part of this delusion is thinking *"I know what's best for my kid."* These people are blind to the lessons inherent in the unique perspectives of adolescence. It is the exceptional adult who truly understands the richness that exists in the lives of young people. For a moment, imagine how you, as an adult, may feel if your ideas and viewpoints were not taken seriously by people you admired and respected? What if your suggestions were trivialized or ridiculed? *Ouch! That hurts!* This is what adults do with teenagers every day. As a result, adolescents feel rejected and/or disenfranchised when their opinions and ideas are minimized or trivialized. Would your self-esteem and confidence grow under these conditions? Of course not!

The exceptional adults who accept the views of teenagers can tell you they have rich and rewarding relationships with these kids. These strong relationships and the power within them are the *"natural consequence"* you receive when you are open to and have the desire to understand your teenager's life experiences.

Handy Insight
Teenagers learn to trust their judgment when their judgments are not judged.

As with any relationship, trust is the foundation. During adolescence, trust is a major casualty in the conflicted relationships between parents and teenagers. As a parent, it's scary and frustrating knowing that your once reliable and cooperative child is now unable or unwilling to do anything without a debate <u>and</u> without a dozen reminders. How can you possibly trust them?

From your teen's perspective, experience has told them that you and most other adults are liars. Why should they trust you? This mutual lack of trust is the basis for most conflicts between parents and teenagers. It's also ironic but true that this loss of trust is fundamental and necessary for teenagers to successfully grow out of this developmental stage and into adulthood.

Communication is critical during adolescence. You need to take the lead and communicate clearly with your teen. First of all, be honest! Be truthful when expressing your feelings, your viewpoints and your concerns, while at the same time remaining open to your teen's perspective. Honesty not only demonstrates good role modeling, but prevents problems later on when your teen eventually discovers that all adults have lied to them. When there is integrity and trust between you and your teen, any problems that arise are easily resolved.

Handy Insight

Be the person you want your teen to become.

Trust grows when communication improves and *Brain Damaged* opens up communication. It's that simple! When you accept the fact that your teenager and teens everywhere are having genuine and real experiences in the world, you send this message to them;

"What goes on in your life, and how you view the world, is important to me."

This is an incredibly powerful thing to say to your kids.

Living and working with teenagers does not have to be a *tug of war* where conflict is seen as a

win-lose situation. Adults win the majority of these battles; oftentimes by pulling rank. (*"I'm the adult and you're the kid, that's why!"*) Because you are now aware of being *Brain Damaged* you can skillfully use the little bits of brain you have left.

You no longer need to pick up the rope, much less tug on it. The *tug of war* is eliminated. Ignorance is the key to understanding who your children are becoming. By not knowing and not pretending to know, you open the door to communication with these precious young people. Even though you are *Brain Damaged,* your teenagers still depend on you to take good care of them. You don't need to know everything to do that.

I've heard many parents say, *"I'll be damned if I'm going to let my kid think he is smarter than me!"* Too late, your kid already is smarter than you. He knows more about the world than you ever did at his age. Every day he is exposed to more sexually graphic and violent images than you were ever exposed to! He or she is proficient with technologies that you are afraid to touch. They have so much to offer us! *Brain Damaged* helps you to get over yourself, your inflated, grandiose sense of importance and open up to the lives of your kids. Kids have it all over adults, and the sad thing is that they could be much further along if adults didn't try to be so darned smart.

If you would rather *not* know about your children's lives, then go right ahead and have all the answers. Go ahead and be the decider; and risk being the divider. Be the *only* one who knows what is best for your kids. Go ahead and deny your children the wisdom they have learned from their experiences in the world. But if you really want to help them, encourage them to use their brain. This is why *Brain Damaged* is brilliant! <u>The less you use your brain the more they use theirs.</u> The less you know, the more they seek answers to their problems. The more they search for answers, the more resourceful they become and the better they get at problem solving. This is good for you and it's good for your kids. I have no idea how this works, I just know it works. Besides, how could I know, I'm *Brain Damaged.*

Adults and adolescents are miles apart in how they perceive the world. There is a huge difference between your world and their world. Your world is old, outdated, uncool, and verrrryyyyy *boring*. Why would they want to be part of your world? Their world is new, exciting, interesting, and dynamic. Their world revolves around their friends, activities, and emotions. Your world usually centers on family and career, and is not likely to be focused on friends. There is no time for friends. You have too many important responsibilities and obligations to attend to; after all you're a grownup!

Developmentally speaking, teenagers have a biological, intellectual and emotional need to be different from you. Until now, you were the person they most wanted to be like. Now you are the person they need to be different from. Let me say this again,

Your teen needs to be different from you.

It's OK and it's necessary. Your kids have important things to take care of as well. They need to get their pinkies wet, dip their toes into the waters of the world, and splash around in it on their own terms. They absolutely need their friends and their friends need them. This is how adolescents manage to accomplish the metamorphosis from child to adult. They need people who see the world from their perspective, and it's not you. Only their friends can do this, along with a few select adults they happen to encounter.

A teenager's world consists of thousands of secret conspiracies where they work out the details of their lives with friends, while adults take a back seat. Their world takes in everything around them and offers it up like a smorgasbord. Your kid picks and chooses amongst all the possible experiences available to them.

Teenagers need to experience the world, period. It is their primary method of learning how to manage their lives and they need to do it without you. So, the more your teen talks with you, the more you will know about their world. This communication is a direct result of being *Brain Damaged*. Here's a little formula you can use to remind you of the relationship between *Brain Damaged* and your teenager's willingness to share openly with you.

$$BD = TS$$
Where: B = Brain
D = Damaged
T = Teen
and
S = Sharing.

In other words:
as Brain Damage increases, Teen Sharing increases.

The more BD, the more TS there will be. It is a direct cause and effect relationship. The good news is this: there are no health risks associated with being *Brain Damaged*.

Handy Insight
If you are Brain Damaged enough, your teen will talk with you about their underlying fears.

As old-fashioned and outdated as your world appears to be to your teen, they still depend upon you to be dependable. You may be old and dusty, but you are also familiar and comfortable in a way that reassures them. Remember this: you *are* the rock! You are the dock that your teens need in order to *shove off* and enter the current of their lives. If you are not solid and grounded in your own life, their attempts to *shove off* will create anxiety and fear. You do <u>not</u> want your children to be *afraid* of their world; you want them to be *masters* of their world.

Nobody knows what will happen when your children are on their own. However, by accepting that you are *Brain Damaged* and being open to their real lives; your children will bring their experiences to you, voluntarily and enthusiastically. Once you have given them all you can give, and you have taught them all you know about living in this world, your kids will enter adulthood knowing that they are important people. They will strike out on their own with confidence and the capacity to succeed in any way they so desire.

Handy Insight

Valuing your teen's life experiences is one of the most important things you can do to ensure their success.

When to be Brain Damaged

There are many opportunities to use *Brain Damaged*, for example, a good time to be *Brain Damaged* is when your kid's friends are around. Allowing their friends to tell you how life is for them will endear you to them, causing you to become *very cool,* plus, you will learn all sorts of things about your kid that otherwise you have no access to. So, *yes,* let your kids' friends hang out at your house. Get to know them and <u>get to know their parents too</u>. This is important.

Talking with other parents will expand your circle of support and bring more energy to the challenging task of raising teenagers. You can *tag team* with other parents and by doing so it is easier to maintain important limits. As you know, your kids will push on and test these limits without thinking about the consequences. Two or more households setting the same limits are much more effective than each household trying to do it on their own.

Towns and neighborhoods used to take on this role, but in today's culture of isolation, it is unusual for families to even know the names of their next door neighbors, much less the families of their kid's friends. Everyone has heard the expression, *"It takes a village to raise a child."* This is exactly what I'm talking about creating. Work together with other parents and you can create your own personal *village* where interested and invested adults come together to support the growth and development of everyone's children.

Handy Insight

Make the effort to get to know the parents of your kid's friends. Create your own village.

Be a good neighbor. Neighbors are a great source of information about your teenager. Even the most *Brain Damaged* parent won't know everything about their kids. Teenagers are very good at keeping things they don't want their parents to know hidden. This is where your neighbors come in. Neighbors can provide that *fast breaking news* only they would know about. Face it, you are not always home when you teenager is home and if you are friends with your neighbors, you will know about any out of the ordinary events they happen to observe. Neighbors can confirm that your son or daughter is doing well while on their own at home, or they can clue you in to a problem that is developing. Connect with your neighbors and if they too have teenagers, all the better. You can keep an eye on their kids as well. It's a win-win-win! You win! Your neighbors win! Your kids win, even if they don't think so.

One thing that has changed drastically since I was a teenager is the involvement of the community in the rearing of children. When I was young and probably when you were young too, our neighbors, store keepers, policemen, and others in the neighborhood were much more involved in the socialization of children. In my small hometown of Montrose, Michigan (pop 2,000 at the time) everyone knew everyone, from the policeman to the man who swept the streets. (Yes, we actually had a street sweeper!) All of the merchants knew who we were and pretty much what we were up to. There was more than one occasion where the watchful eye of one of the townspeople kept me from making a poor decision.

These community members modeled for me different ways of being grown up and gave me different adults to relate to. This experience was invaluable in my social and moral development. I wish it were more prevalent in today's culture. I now live in a large city and kids still live in neighborhoods, cruise the local shops, and hang out together on the streets. However, I rarely see a merchant or a patron say anything to a kid much less comment on how they are behaving (good or bad).

I don't know why we are so indifferent to our children, but this lack of interaction between adults in the community and your children can undermine the very social skills you want your kids to develop. So, the next time you are out and about shopping or running errands and you see a teenager, be bold, be courageous and give that kid something to think about whether it is a compliment, a reprimand or a nugget of your wisdom. You will have done a favor for both of you.

How to Apply Your Damaged Brain

Brain Damaged can be misused as with any of the Ten Tips. You must be clear on this; *Brain Damaged* is *not* about faking ignorance. For example, a parent may ask their son or daughter, *"How was math class today?"* after the school called to report an absence. Your kid will see right through you. They are way too smart for that and they know you much better than you think. They know when you are not being sincere. They know when you are faking it.

Being *Brain Damaged* relieves you of the pressure of having to know more than your children. It's not about being right! It's about being there. As a parent your job is to encourage your kid to use their brain so they can stop being dependent upon your brain (even more irony). The goal of *Brain Damaged* is to maximize the use of your teenager's brain and to minimize the use of yours. Don't you want your kids to think for themselves? Of course you do! But for them to be good at it, they need lots and lots of practice. Don't let your damaged brain butt into their training exercises. Let them wrestle with life. Let them exercise their brain.

Now go ahead, permit yourself to be *Brain Damaged* and let your inner idiot emerge. You will be surprised at how much your child knows and how capable and competent he or she already is.

Be sincere when you ask questions. Be curious and genuinely interested when you ask for more details. If you don't understand what is going on, then ask. If you are sincere and genuine, most teens will tell you what is going on. Being successfully *Brain Damaged* means you are motivated by curiosity with a genuine and sincere interest in your teenager's world.

Handy Insight

Never, never, ever demand your teen tell you anything! Demanding compliance from anyone is bullying and a misuse of your power as a parent. Kids have the same right as you do to remain silent.

How do you know when you're Brain Damaged?

Don't worry about this, your son or daughter will tell you in very clear terms when you are B*rain Damaged.* You might get the classic *eye roll* or a combination of the *eye roll* and the *heavy sigh.* There are also many nonverbal signals that teens send out when they have encountered *Brain Damaged* adults. Some other signs include, but are not limited to:

- Staring at you dumbstruck, sometimes with their eyes crossed

- Saying the word "Duhhhhh......!"

- Walking out of the room silently (occurs rarely)

- Walking out of the room mumbling (predictable)

- Storming out of the room ranting (occurs often)

- Placing the thumb and index finger to their forehead, forming an "L" (often combined with the eye roll)

- Throwing their hands over their head and mumbling under their breaths while walking around in circles

- Stating as fact, *"You're hopeless!"*

- Stating as fact, *"You don't get it!"*

- Stating as fact, *"Well, thanks a lot!"* (implied "for nothing")

The list can go on and on and on. Please take a few minutes to write down some of the common responses to being *Brain Damaged* in your household:

When I'm declared to be *Brain Damaged* my teen will:

_____

_____

_____

or they will:

_____

_____

_____

or they will even:

_____

_____

_____

It is important to note that according to your teen, there is a hierarchy of *Brain Damaged* people. Below is a sample of how your teen ranks you, their friend's parents and other groups of adults on this scale.

- My parents are completely *Brain Damaged.*

- My teachers are very *Brain Damaged*; but not as bad as my parents.

- My neighbors are *Brain Damaged* too, but not as bad as my parents or my teachers.

- The parents of my friends are slightly *Brain Damaged*, but only when I'm with my friends.

- My friends are not *Brain Damaged* at all, well maybe one or two of them.

- People between the ages of 18 to 24 are brilliant, geniuses and Gods

Situations where it is to your advantage to be *Brain Damaged*:

- When your teen expresses a strong emotion, positive or negative

- If your child uses an expletive -!@#$%! (I know this is rare, but I'm sure it happens)

- When your child is late getting home

- When your teen is avoiding chores, homework, avoiding you, but especially if they are avoiding a friend

- When your teen yells at you

- When your teen yells at a brother or sister

- When report cards come out

- When your teen comes to you with a problem (Do not under any circumstance try to solve the problem.)

- When your teen breaks a family rule they've agreed to

- When your teen becomes a permanently fixed object, but still has vital signs.

- And on and on and on ...

I love being *Brain Damaged*. It allows me to be in a position of trust with the teenagers who have risked it all to share their world with me, an adult. I'm not just an adult; I'm a "shrink". But, as good a tip as *Brain Damaged* is, it is only a tiny piece of the puzzle in the challenges you face with your teen.

Parenting does not have to be complicated. It doesn't need to be stressful. It doesn't need to be difficult. In fact raising a teenager can be downright joyful, if you choose it to be. The best interventions are:

1. Simple
2. Easy to use and
3. Effective.

Brain Damaged meets all these criteria. So why not give it a whirl. Take it for a test drive and have fun being *Brain Damaged*. Using this tip with any of the other tips will increase their power three fold. Really! Now get out there and forget something.

Ten Tips to Tame Your Teen

Chapter 2

The Hit and Run

"It is hard to convince a high-school student that he will encounter a lot of problems more difficult than those of algebra and geometry." ~Edgar W. Howe

The Hit and Run is a perfect tool to use when you need to confront your teen. You want to make your point in a clear and concise way AND avoid an argument at the same time. No matter what problem they have, *The Hit and Run* sets the stage for their success. Be crystal clear and keep your message short and sweet! Follow the steps below for a perfect *Hit and Run*.

1) Know <u>exactly</u> what you want to say.

2) Go to where your teen is taking up space.

3) Get their attention.

4) Make your statement (once only).

5) Leave immediately.

After you leave, your teen can't argue with you and avoid dealing with what you've just said. *The Hit and Run* gives your teen a chance to think about the point you made. Before exiting, be sure to tell them, *"We will discuss this later, today."* In the meantime prepare yourself to work *with* your teen to help them address the issue. <u>Follow-up is critical, do not put it off!</u>

Do not skip any of the above steps and do them in order. Commit them to memory and use *The Hit and Run* so often that it becomes second nature. However, before you even think about using *The Hit and Run*, you must know your reasons for jumping into a problem your teen has created. Ask yourself these questions:

1) How am I feeling about my teen right now?

2) What is their responsibility for this problem?

3) What concerns do I have about my teen's ability to solve this problem?

4) What do they need in order to solve this problem?

5) What if they do nothing?

6) What part, if any, do I have in this problem?

7) What do I want my child to learn from this experience?

Make sure you know the answers to these questions and eliminate all negative thoughts about your teen's ability to solve this problem. Believe in your teen and you super-size *The Hit and Run*.

Making the *Hit* is easy and the *Run* gives you time to prepare for Stage 2 of this tip: *The Meeting*. This is the most important part of *The Hit and Run*. These questions prepare you for this all-important meeting of the minds. When you know your answers to these questions you are prepared to manage this encounter. Be aware of your thoughts, feelings, and perceptions and communicate them clearly to your teen at the appropriate time.

Handy Insight
Don't wait until the progress report to learn your teen is having problems at school.

The parents in this cartoon have taken timely and necessary action and they are prepared for *The Meeting*. Unfortunately, they've been ignoring some obvious signs of trouble and were shocked when they received their daughter's progress. Look at the cartoon again. What evidence do you see that suggests this teen is having trouble with organization? If you answered *"her room is a mess"*, then you have very good instincts!

You might be saying to yourself right now, *"Yeah, so what? My kid's room is worse than that and they get straight A's!"* This may be true in your case, but normally, when a kid's room is chaotic then their life is chaotic. Living like a pig is not normal or healthy for anyone! Really? Yes, really. A messy room can indicate that your child's life is out of control. Take a moment now and think about anything in your home that may indicate a potential problem. Is there a connection between the condition of your kid's room and their ability to organize their life? I'm guessing there is.

I'm not using your kid's room as an example because I want you to get them to clean it up; there are plenty of books out there to tell you how to do that. What I want you to do is increase your awareness of the subtle signs that your teen is sending to you. Secretly, they <u>want</u> you to notice these signs. They <u>need</u> you to see these signs because they do not yet feel confident when facing personal and worldly problems. Of course, your teen will deny this, but they do depend upon your experience to help them solve problems. After all you've been solving problems all of their lives. The challenge for you now is to know when you are overly involved in their process.

Handy Insight

Power struggles are evidence that you are taking ownership for your children's problems.

Question: *"How many teenagers does it take to screw in a light bulb?*

Answer: *Only one, but the teen has to really want to change the bulb."*

Isn't this true for all of us? You don't get much done unless you <u>want</u> to get it done! Even the most distasteful of tasks are completed because you <u>want</u> them completed <u>and</u> you have chosen to take action.

When I was a teen, my main job around the house was to mow the lawn every week. This was no lightweight yard, mind you. We lived on a quarter acre and there were plenty of obstacles. Then one day, as I finished the job, I noticed something. I liked the way the lawn looked. After admiring my work for a long time I asked the gang to come over and play baseball on our beautiful newly mowed lawn. My backyard served as the neighborhood baseball diamond.

Today, I don't like mowing the lawn any more than I did then, but I still like the way it looks when I'm finished. It is this intrinsic pleasure of a job well done that we need to instill in our youth. Expecting your teen to help out in the family <u>and</u> you holding them accountable, it affects them for life, in a good way. A job well done is a cornerstone for a quality life.

Most of the time, you trust yourself and your ability to come up with solutions to the problems you encounter. This trust permits you to explore all of the possible solutions. Trusting yourself also lets you ask for help when you need it. You know it is not up to you to solve their problems, but your teen doesn't have a clue. So, what do you do?

This is why *The Hit and Run* is such a valuable addition to your toolbox of parenting skills. The *Hit and Run* creates an opportunity for your son or daughter to take responsibility for their problems. This realization can only be realized if you have *The Meeting* as soon as possible after *The Hit and Run*. Here are some reasons why following-up is the most critical part of this tip.

1) It tells your teen you mean business.

2) You establish the expectation that they take this problem seriously.

3) You give them the message that you believe in them.

4) You confirm that they are important to you.

Now comes the hard part for most parents. It is absolutely critical to emotionally detach from any expectation that your teen, in the meanwhile, has been working on the problem. There is a good chance they have not done anything since *The Hit and Run*. As the adult, you can only give them a chance to practice critical thinking skills. This doesn't mean they will. How your teen responds to *The Hit and Run* will be unique to them. Often, however a teenager's first response to this tip is to do nothing. If they ignore it, the problem may go away, right? <u>Don't take this lack of initiative personally</u>.

It may be frustrating to learn that your teen has not given any thought to the problem, but do not despair because this is often the case when parents try something new. New interventions often don't appear to work right away. There is no need to be frustrated. Simply tell them again and remind your teen that you expect them to come up with a plan. Then give them 30 minutes to work on it and reconvene. If there is still no response then it suggests the problem may not be what you think it is. This is where *Brain Damaged* comes in handy.

When your teen does nothing; a pattern I call *The Passive Trap*, it can be really frustrating for parents. Frustration, disappointment and even anger are common responses to a teen's unwillingness to solve a problem or take on more responsibility.

"Don't fall for it."

This is a trap! The problem is <u>theirs</u> and if you take over, they will not learn the lesson. So, what do you do if your child hasn't given any serious thought to the problem? You do nothing. Not the kind of nothing that leaves your teen hanging out there on their own, but the kind of nothing that opens up a dialogue. Since this is a new approach for you too, it will take practice to be good at it. Remain detached and be clear about what you expect from your teen. In addition, if your teen is used to you solving their problems, they will need time to come up with their own solutions. Be patient with yourself and with your teen.

If your teen does not come up with a plan then use *Brain Damaged* before you jump in and take over. Think about it, doesn't it confuse you that your brilliant child hasn't budged to solve this problem? It doesn't take her long to come up with reasons to go to the mall. If you are feeling confused then you are using the tip correctly. Confusion is expected at times like this. Go with it. It is also the time to be curious about what is preventing your child from being proactive. *Brain Damaged* helps you to do this and is a perfect follow up for *The Hit and Run*. You can say,

"I'm really confused about what is keeping you from taking care of this problem."

Curiosity opens up a dialogue with your teen and with support she will come up with some good ideas.

While attending graduate school at California State University in Sacramento, I worked at the Sacramento Children's Home, a residential treatment facility that has been around for more than 100 years. They have excellent programs for kids without parents, or parents who cannot care for them. The majority of these teenagers have a history of abuse and neglect. Many are severely emotionally disturbed, in special education, and on medication. They needed a tremendous amount of support to manage their behavior, much less manage their lives. Many of these teenagers were in family therapy and counseling for the abuse and neglect that occurred in their lives.

On the campus of the Children's Home, there were 4 cottages with 12-13 adolescents in each. All of the kids were between 13 and 18 years-old. Did I mention these cottages were also coed? Imagine that! Six boys and six girls living together. We needed structure. Structure is important for all kids and at the Children's Home, Saturday morning was the designated cleaning day and each resident had specific duties to perform before they could go outside and play. Each cottage was thoroughly inspected with bedrooms, bathrooms, and common areas inspected and points awarded based on the quality of their work.

My shift started on Friday afternoon and ended Saturday afternoon. It was called a *sleepover* shift. On Saturday mornings, as I prepared breakfast, I supervised the cleanup. The residents were not allowed to go outside until their job was inspected and *"checked off."* I was not the inspector, but I was the pre-inspector and held each resident accountable for doing a job well done. In other words, if they passed my inspection they would pass the official inspection. Imagine how much energy it takes to prepare breakfast for 12 severely emotionally disturbed teenagers AND support them completing their chores in a timely manner. The sooner they met my standards, the sooner they could go out and play.

The Hit and Run was an extremely valuable tool on Saturday mornings. I had the power to grant the residents access to the recreation hall. The kids knew what was expected of them, but needed lots of support. With consistency and patience most of them adjusted to the routines and structure that was in place to help them create a sense of order out of their chaotic lives.

There were some residents, however, who struggled with keeping order of any kind in their lives and had significant difficulty with structure. They grew up in really chaotic environments and appeared to be attracted to chaos, even eerily comfortable with chaos. These kids had difficulty with the simplest of tasks and became frustrated very easily, oftentimes *blowing out* and spending much of their morning in the *sitting chair,* a place where they could be supervised as they calmed down. When calm, we would try it again, hopefully with better results.

These kids required additional patience and acceptance of their process. It was difficult for them to maintain order in their rooms, much less order in their lives. Using *The Hit and Run* allowed me to be clear about my expectation and simultaneously give them the time and space to accomplish their tasks. Sometimes I repeated the expectation over and over and over. This required patience and persistence. Just like you.

Before they ended up at the Children's Home these kids were repeatedly told they were incapable and incompetent. Every day I reminded them that they <u>are</u> capable and competent. I trusted them to dig down deep and move, step by step, inch by inch, toward their goal. In this case their goal was not necessarily the satisfaction of a job well done, but to go outside and play as soon as possible. I learned early on that getting frustrated and angry with these kids only pushed buttons and caused more problems.

Occasionally a resident refused to do anything. They refused to do their job; they refused to make their bed and so on. That's right; it's the old *Passive Trap*. <u>Passive is really powerful</u>. When a kid dug in their heels it was very distressful to the other residents because points are lost when jobs are not completed. Nearly everyone attempted to convince, coerce or threaten these kids into doing their part. The *Passive Trap* is so powerful that some residents even offered to do the job for them.

If your child avoids taking action to solve a problem, then there are underlying fears that are keeping your teenager from moving forward. Often you may experience their fears as anger, resentment, hostility, avoidance, depression, defiance or all of the above. Meanwhile, exclamations such as, *"School sucks!"* and *"I don't care"* are screamed out along with looks that can kill.

Comments like this are serious indications that your teen is having problems. *Don't* power struggle with them. From their perspective, they are in a life and death battle for ultimate power and control over their life. *Don't* get sucked in. All you want them to do is take responsibility and do something. *Be patient*, it's not that easy for them.

Handy Insight

The more out of control a person is the more they try to control others.

This Handy Insight says that behaviors such as blaming, guilt tripping, threatening, yelling or bribing are all efforts to control another. These methods bring only short term gains, if any gains at all. Be aware of any controlling behavior you may have and let it go. Make sure you are not the one who is out of control.

For the kids at the Children's Home, acting out was how they got attention from the adults in their life, and boy, did it work. They got attention alright, but it was angry and hurtful attention. I noticed that when a staff member became frustrated and angry with a resident, this resident felt a combination of anxiety AND power; a familiar power that often provoked adults to harm them verbally, emotionally and/or physically. This kind of power has disastrous results. Don't let anger be the only response you or your teen have when faced with interpersonal conflict. At the Children's Home, I could not huff and puff my way through these mornings, I needed finesse, I needed some tools and thus the seed for the Ten Tips was sowed.

Every morning each resident was required to make their beds, fold their clothes and put them in the dressers or hang them up in their closets. Clutter of any kind was not acceptable. The older teens kept their rooms in pretty good order, but for some of the younger ones, their rooms deteriorated over time, sometimes within hours or even minutes after the Saturday morning *check off.* Most of these kids grew up in chaos and disorder until they arrived at The Children's Home. Chaos was all they knew. Over time, I learned that the condition of their room was a good barometer of the condition of their life. If the room was reasonably tidy then the resident was calmer, more in control of themselves and they were able to manage their lives relatively well.

So, the next time you get frustrated with your son or daughter because of the nuclear explosions and chemistry experiments going on in their room, take a moment and consider what may be fueling this pigsty. The chaos in their room may be a clue as to how they are experiencing life. As you saw in the previous cartoon, the parents are very clear in their feelings (*"We are very disappointed....."*) AND their expectations (*"We expect you to figure out ..."*) and they state their intention to follow up on this concern (*"We will get together after dinner...."*). When you use *The Hit and Run,* follow up is essential. But first, let's get out of their room as fast as possible!!! Go Now! Don't hesitate!

The Hit and Run is wonderful because, by leaving, it follows that if you aren't in the same room as your teen, they can't argue with you. By the time you get together later on, the strong emotions will have calmed down and your teen may actually have put some thought into fixing the problem. Be pleasantly surprised if this happens and talk about how the plan can be maintained and how you can be supportive.

It is important to know what is going on in your teenager's world and to pay attention to how they are responding to their life experiences. Take a moment now and go look at your kid's room. Don't judge it, just look at it. What do you see? Order? Chaos? Something in between order and chaos? Is your teen calm, anxious, hysterical? Is their personal life orderly or as chaotic as their room?

Fun Facts about Adolescents

In studies by David Elkind at the Department of Child Study, Tufts University along with Bowen, Inhelder and Piaget, it was noted, "Adolescent argumentativeness, self-consciousness, and idealism are related to their newfound capacity for abstract thought."

As this fun fact notes, teenagers tend to be argumentative. (Just in case you haven't noticed.) Their tendency towards opposition and defiance can be traced back to their brain, yes their expanding brain. Their inability to cooperate at times merely reflects their effort to develop abstract reasoning skills. This helps them become better thinkers and better problem solvers. So the next time your teenager argues with you, smile at them knowing that that they are getting better at abstract reasoning.

What happens <u>after</u> *The Hit and Run* and <u>before</u> *The Meeting*? Nothing happens. That's right, nothing. Leave your kid alone. Do not talk with them about the problem. Do not check in with them about their progress. Do not share your hopes and fears with them. If you must talk with someone, talk with your spouse or partner, and if they are not available then call a friend. (It's OK to reach out; after all, you can't do this parenting thing alone.) Let your kid think for a while and come up with some ideas. They <u>will</u> work out a solution because they prefer to solve the problem than experience the consequences of not solving the problem. They really do love you and they really don't want to disappoint you.

While you are giving time and space to your teen what's the atmosphere like in your house? Are you walking on pins and needles? Is your teen sullen and hostile towards you? Are they holed up in their room? Is your teen planning to run away to the circus and packing a suitcase at this very moment? Any of these events can derail you from your purpose. And what's your purpose? <u>The purpose of *The Hit and Run* is to help your teenager engage their brain so they can develop critical thinking and problem solving skills.</u>

If there is so much tension in the house that nobody says anything to anybody until *The Meeting*, that's okay. Give the tension time to wear off. Do not postpone the meeting just because your kid is mad at you. Your challenge is to remain cool, calm and collected.

Do whatever you need to do to calm your nerves and take care of yourself. Practice deep breathing, meditate, do yoga, go for a run, or bake some cookies. But do what it takes to reclaim your peace of mind. You are going to need to be calm and in control of yourself for *The Meeting*. If you remain calm and peaceful, all will be well. Oh, yeah, make sure that you AND your teen, get something to eat <u>before</u> *The Meeting*. Do not attempt this on an empty stomach.

Speaking of eating, sharing a meal together is a time to reconnect and a time to enjoy each other. Make eating together a sacred and pleasant time for your family. Dinnertime is not the time to talk about problems. So, what *do* you talk about at dinner if you can't talk about the day's problems? What do you normally talk about with your kids at dinner? Do you even eat dinner together? If your family eats dinner together, then make it a time to relax. Take care of business after dinner. If your family is too busy to eat dinner together, then make time. Not eating together leads to other problems.

There is no hard and fast rule about how to use any of the Ten Tips. In fact the more creative you are with these tips, the more effective you will be. The way your family deals with each other is unique, so when using *The Hit and Run* or any of the Ten Tips focus on your family's strengths and build on what's already there.

THE MEETING

There are two things to keep in mind during *The Meeting:*

1) This is the time to discuss your concerns.

2) It's the time to talk about how capable and competent your teenager is.

3) It is also the time to hold them accountable.

Statements like,

"We are concerned that something may be going on with you and we want you to know that we love you and we are here for you. We know you can do better in school."

or

"I love you and I know you can succeed at anything you choose. Now what are you going to do about these grades?"

The goal of *The Meeting* is to formulate the plan, a plan that your amazing teenager creates. Your job is to create a safe environment and your teen's job is to create the plan. Your teen needs to feel safe before they will tell you what's really going on. They need to know that their thoughts and feelings will be taken seriously. Your job is to listen and to not judge. In a nutshell, your job is to ask questions that help your teen pull their plan together.

<u>Do not</u> offer suggestions or direct your teen in any way. Keep in mind that you are *Brain Damaged* and besides, you want your teen to use <u>their</u> brain. In this way they learn to think independently. Isn't that what you want?

Teenagers <u>do</u> want to do well in school and they <u>do</u> want their parents to be proud of them. If they are not doing well, there is a reason for it. If your son or daughter is having a hard time with school, then take steps to provide more academic and emotional support. This support can include any one or more of the following:

- Meeting with school personnel

- Hiring a tutor

- Testing for possible learning disabilities

- Counseling if there appears to be emotional problems

- More family engagement. This tells your teen they are part of the family.

Your teen may need a tutor, an educational or psychological assessment. They may even counseling, but mostly they need to know that you love and approve of them, no matter what they say or do.

Do not rule out the possibility of alcohol or drug abuse. It is critical to confront any substance use. It tells your teen you care about them and you love them unconditionally. This cannot be overstated. Do not compromise their safety.

Handy Insight
WHOSE PROBLEM IS IT?
If you take responsibility for your teenager's problem, they will expect you to solve it for them. It is their job to solve their problem!

If you repeatedly get angry with your teen and engage in power struggles, then STOP immediately and look at yourself. Identify at least 3 reasons why you, the grownup, are getting into power struggles with a child; a big child, but a child nonetheless. Your teen does not have the power to force you into a power struggle or cause an argument. You participate voluntarily. <u>You have a choice</u>. This doesn't mean you pull rank and act like you know what you're talking about; it simply means to respond to your teenager like they are worthy of respect. You know, the way you might talk with someone at work or the way you might respond to a friend that you're frustrated with. When you take responsibility for your part in a power struggle the power struggle ends.

I am not saying you can't ever be angry with your teen; however, I am encouraging you to use *The Hit and Run* before you pull your hair out and start to scream. Practice *The Hit and Run* a few times before you reach the end of your rope. Don't wait until you can't take it anymore. Use it on little things. It's a great way to get your point across, quickly and efficiently. Plus, you set the stage for your teen to learn how to solve even the biggest of the biggest problems.

After you have some experience with *The Hit and Run* on negative events, try it on positive events. Take a moment and think about a time when you were enjoying your teen, really enjoying them, a time when you were loving and appreciating them for being the person they are. This is the perfect time to give them a *Hit and Run.* Now that you are all filled up with these wonderful, loving feelings go to them and say,

"You know I can't get over how much you have grown up recently. I am so proud of you."

Then walk away. There is no need to follow-up with this type of *Hit and Run*. Let that rattle around in their head for a while. If your teen is not there, call them up and say it over the phone, then hang up.

Handy Insight

No matter what happens to your teen, remember, it is not happening to you.

Let me ask a few things. How does <u>their</u> school performance affect <u>your</u> life? Does the condition of their room or the friends they hang out with have a lasting effect on <u>your</u> life? Probably not, but school and friends do have lasting effects on your teenager's life. I know at times you have concerns and with good reason, but if you take over the problem, then you undermine your teen's development and you set up a power struggle.

They know it's their problem and they know it's their responsibility, even if they blame you or others. And believe it or not, they really do want to solve these problems themselves. There are times when your man-child or woman-child needs and wants you to help, but cannot bring themselves to ask. Even though your teen thinks you are *Brain Damaged*, at a deep, deep level they know you have solutions to their problems. At the same time, they secretly want you to take care of them, like when they were small and you kissed the boo boo to make it all better. Now say goodnight and don't forget to leave the light on in the hallway.

The Hit and Run is versatile and can be used with a wide range of problems that parents of adolescents are faced with. In fact, it can be used for nearly any situation.

Ten Tips to Tame Your Teen

The Hit and Run is highly effective with:

- Family Relationships
- Household Chores
- School Responsibilities
- Boyfriends/Girlfriends/Lack of either
- Good friends/Bad friends
- Lack of friends/Too many friends
- No Job/Job/No Job, again . . .
- Alcohol and Drug use or abuse
- And the list goes on…..

Use this tip liberally, especially in combination with *Brain Damaged* and before you know it, that once *"lazy, good for nothing kid"* will surprise you, in a good way.

The Hit and Run

Ten Tips to Tame Your Teen

Chapter 3
Two Little Words

*"I've learned that although it's hard to admit it,
I'm secretly glad my parents are strict." ~ Child
Age 15*

Two Little Words works great to hold teenagers accountable. *Two Little Words* create opportunities for teens to take responsibility and do what they said they would do. These *Two Little Words*, <u>nevertheless</u> and <u>regardless</u>, allow you to listen carefully to your teen, genuinely feel empathy for them and say,

"I'm really sorry that the swim party has come up so suddenly, but <u>nevertheless</u>, we agreed on Tuesday that you would clean your room before going anywhere today"
or
"<u>Regardless</u> of the fact that you have been very helpful over the past few days, you are still grounded until Friday."

How many times has this happened to you? Everyone in the family agrees; Saturday night is going to be family night. The agenda is set, the menu is planned, the games and DVDs have been picked out, when suddenly you hear a noise coming from the back door. It's rattling like someone is urgently trying to get in. Your heart jumps and you look at each other. It's your son and he nearly trips over the dog as he rushes in yelling, *"Mom! Dad! There's an emergency!"* *"Oh my gosh . . ."* you shriek! *"What's the matter?"* *"It's Tommy's birthday and he's invited me to his party!!!"* (Pant, pant, pant) You say, *"That's great, when's the party?"* *"It's tonight!"* he says, with wide eyed excitement. He pants, *"Can I go, huh? Can I go?"*

You look at each other, and then look at your son. He's anxiously waiting your answer, *"Huh, can I go, can I? Everyone's going to be there! Pleeeeaaasssse?"* You look at each other again and both of you say, in two part harmony, *"It's a shame that Tommy didn't give you more notice; and we know you really, really want to go, nevertheless, we've all agreed that tonight is going to be family night!"*

Dad says, *"I do believe you were there on Tuesday when we made that decision."* Your son then says, *"But this is important, I get to see you guys all of the time and besides it's his*

birthday." You go on to say, *"We know how important this is to you and you have every right to be disappointed, but regardless of the circumstances, you have a commitment to your family. Now go call Tommy and tell him that you have other plans. Don't worry; we'll have lots of fun."* He grunts and then sulks off to call his friend.

Remembering is the key to super-sizing this tip. It is critical to remember what life was like when you were an adolescent. If you can't remember your teenage experiences or you choose not, you will not be able to empathize with your teen. Therefore, I strongly recommend you take some time and go through old family photo albums and reminisce about your life as a teenager. Re-examine your family dynamics, your friendships, your memories, and the feelings you felt. I'm not talking about a brief glimpse back in time. I am talking about a heartfelt search to reacquaint yourself with your experiences as a teenager.

When you remember what life was like for you as a teenager, you connect with what is currently happening with your teen and how they feel about it. There is no right or wrong way to do this and I guarantee you will gain valuable insights into your son or daughter's life. This act alone will increase your empathy quotient tenfold. Who knows, it could be fun to make your search a family activity. It's a wonderful opportunity for your kids to learn new things about you. Share your life story with your children. Don't be a stranger to them and they won't become strangers to you.

Fun Facts about Adolescents

In her article, "Setting Limits for Your Teen", Kathleen McCoy, Ph.D. urges parents to remember that teens have mixed feelings about limits that mirror their developmental position between childhood and adulthood: while they may balk at limits, argue with you and claim to have the maturity to make all of their own choices, they feel quietly reassured when parents step in and let them know what they expect of them. Deep down, most teenagers see limits as reassuring, as a sign of ongoing parental protection, and as proof that their parents really care.

Take a moment right now and think back to your own adolescence and the life you left so far behind.

- Imagine urgently running up to your parents, excited and anticipating all the fun at the party you have just been invited to. You pop the question, *"Can I go? Everyone is going to be there!"*

- What are you feeling at that moment?

- How much anticipation and excitement do you have?

- How nervous are you about asking permission?

- What makes this party so important?

- How important is family night compared to going to this party?

How did your parents respond?

- Did they let you go to the party, even though previous plans were made?

- Did they try to hold you to your commitment, but you managed to talk them out of it and go to the party?

- Did your parents hold you to your commitment and instead of going to the party; you stayed home with the family?

- Did your parents disagree with each other? Did this disagreement cause an argument between them? Did this work in your favor because in the heat of battle, you snuck out and went to the party anyway?

- Were your parents even home? Did you find a note on the kitchen counter saying, *"We are at the Hobart's for dinner, there are leftovers in the fridge, don't wait up for us, we love you."* This is great! Now you can go to the party.

When you remember what it was like for you as a teenager, you can respond to your teen with empathy.

According to Webster's Online Dictionary, empathy is: *the capacity to recognize or understand another's state of mind or emotion. It is often characterized as the ability to "put oneself into another's shoes", or to in some way experience the outlook or emotions of another being within oneself. It may be described metaphorically as an emotional kind of resonance or mirroring.*

Empathy allows you to feel what your teen is feeling. When you are empathetic you make an emotional connection with your teen, frequently it's not necessary to say anything. When you are connected, being there is enough. They feel your presence and this comforts them.

Do not to let your inner parent convince you that you were different than your teen. While it is true that the world is very different today, the needs of teenagers have remained the same. What you needed then and what they need now are the same things.

One hundred fifty years ago, people depended on horses as their main mode of transportation. A hundred years ago the telephone was just beginning to be used in households. Fifty years ago, rock and roll burst onto the scene and the sexual revolution captivated the youth while Bob Dylan sang, *"The times, they are a changin'."* Actually, the times are always a changin'.

Kids 150 years ago were already living and working in the adult world by the time they were teenagers. Many of them were also married and starting families. A century and a half ago children were seen as a labor source and there were practical reasons for families being large. My, how times have changed!

Handy Insight

*Don't do anything for your teen that they
can and need to do for themselves.*

This Handy Insight is talking about things
like cleaning up after them, washing their
clothes, cooking all of their meals or doing their
chores. They are in training to be an adult and
they need all the practice they can get. They
need to do these things for themselves and they
are not going to do them perfectly. You weren't
so good the first time you cooked a meal either.
They don't need to clean that shower perfectly,
make that bed perfectly or mow that lawn
perfectly either. You don't have to be perfect
and neither does your teen. Now doesn't that
feel good? All you need to do is be *good
enough.* Good enough is just that, good enough.
Parenting is not an exact science. Perfect parents
do not exist. Plus you may have noticed lately,
that your perfect children have turned into
perfect Tasmanian devils. It makes no sense to
try to be a perfect parent when good enough is
all it takes. Somehow, if you give your kids
what they truly need, they will become amazing
adults in spite of you. Remember, <u>you are
humans raising humans.</u> Don't take the job too
seriously.

Mistakes are part of everyone's growth and
development. Your mistakes are yours to grow
from and your teens' mistakes are theirs to grow
from. Learning from our mistakes is one of the
indicators that we are *growing up.* Everyone has
heard the saying,

"Insanity is doing the same thing over and over while expecting different results."

If you do not learn from your mistakes, you will keep doing the same old things and getting the same old results. If you insist on perfection, then you are setting yourself up. Forget about any need you have to be right. Let your teen be right once in a while. Having to be right alienates you from your teen at a time when they need you as a resource, even though you are *Brain Damaged.*

I've heard many parents say in defense of their harsh reactions to their kids, *"My parents spanked, beat, yelled and cursed at me and I turned out alright. Spare the rod, spoil the child."* What are they thinking? How can they see this as a good thing? What kind of logic is being used to justify a parent's out-of-control behavior? As a parent you have an obligation to teach your kids how to solve problems and resolve conflict, not contribute to their problems or create conflict with harsh words and corporeal punishment. Many of you may have grown up in households where your parents were physically, emotionally or mentally abusive. It is important as a parent, that you learn the lessons presented to you by this experience. If you were abused as a child it is your responsibility to stop the cycle of abuse. *Ten Tips to Tame Your Teen* helps you to do that.

Handy Insight
Life as an adolescent can get out of control quickly. They need you to be cool, calm, and collected.

Nevertheless and regardless helps you to stay focused on the limits that have been set and reminds your teen of prior commitments. This tip is a simple and effective way to keep your cool and make it clear to your teen that they cannot persuade you to change your mind. There is no argument and you feel no frustration. Even if your teen becomes angry and frustrated, there is no need for you to lose your cool. It's not your problem, but an empathic response along with one of the *Two Little Words* does the job. Your teen soon learns that you are committed to the agreement and no amount of persuasion or coercion will change anything. This is what being a good enough parent is all about. It is important also to be flexible if there are sound reasons to do so. A good enough parent is like an oak tree, strong yet flexible.

You are probably all too familiar with the emotional roller coaster that earmarks the adolescent experience. Feelings are the common denominator for you and your teen. Raising adolescents is a perpetual deja vú because you have felt what they are feeling now. Remember the boy who wanted to go to the party? Like you, the boy probably felt excitement, anticipation, anxiety, and then disappointment, in that order. As you remember your own experience, how did you feel as you approached your parents about "bailing" on a family activity in favor of a night out with your friends? You too may have felt excitement (about being invited to a party), anticipation (of all the fun you were going to have), anxiety (about asking for your parents' permission), and disappointment (when your parents held you to your agreement).

Saying *no* is important, but it is important to say *no* in a way that acknowledges the emotions that your son or daughter is having at this gut wrenching, heartbreaking, clock striking midnight moment. The power of empathy cannot be overstated. Your kids will not only get the message that you mean what you say, but they will also know that you understand and appreciate their dilemma.

By being empathetic you feel what your child is feeling. You connect to their sense of urgency. You can be genuine, caring and understanding in your response. They have their own reasons why this party is important. The more you empathize with their desire, the more your teen will accept the limit you are setting. Even though they may act like this as the worst possible thing you could do to them, they will, n*evertheless* survive, just as you survived the very same experience when you were their age.

When you remember, you become aware of the reasons why they are soooo... excited about going to a party (you've been there), you know about their anticipation (you've been there), you know how anxious they are to ask for your permission (you've been there) and you know their disappointment when you tell them no. You've been there and you survived.

Nobody wants their child to go behind their backs and sneak out to go places. These children often grow up and become sneaky, conniving, and manipulative adults. When you hold your teenager accountable, you give them an opportunity to feel these uncomfortable feelings and by doing so, you help them to grow up. In this situation, by teaching accountability you also teach them the value and power of their word. When you use the *Two Little Words* you are contributing to the growth and development of adolescents who become reliable and trustworthy.

The most powerful way to teach this, of course is by example. If you are in the habit of breaking promises and commitments to your children, *Nevertheless* and *Regardless* will have little or no impact. In fact, your teenager will use your behavior as an excuse to avoid taking responsibility for themselves. Has your teen ever snapped at you, *"You don't keep your promises either!"* If your word can't be trusted then they will not value commitment. If this is the case, you can use *Two Little Words* as much as you want and it will not be effective.

Your challenge is to BE the man or woman you want your son or daughter to become. Be the kind of man you want your daughter to fall in love with. Be the kind of woman you want your son to fall in love with. Speak with integrity and act with integrity. Hold yourself accountable to yourself and with others. Be careful to manage your commitments wisely and always do your best. When you do the best you can, you model that behavior to your children, which teaches them to do their best. Can we ask any more of our young people?

The behavior you expect from your teenaged son or daughter needs to be modeled by you to the best of your ability. Not perfectly, just the best you can. Do not expect perfection from yourself or your kids. Behave in ways that communicates to your teen that doing their best and making mistakes helps them to grow. I love hearing parents say to their teens,

"That's OK, you did the best you could and I'm proud of you."

This is a very powerful thing to say to your kids. Say it often, but when you say it, <u>always</u> be sincere. Imagine how your teenager will react when you look at them and say, *"I'm sorry; I'm doing the best I can."* What will they say after you admit to being less than perfect?

Handy Insight
Never promise your teen more than you can give.

Limit setting is not just for kids. It's for you too. I frequently encourage parents to promise no more than they can deliver. Then make every effort possible to make good on the promise. If you make a promise, then keep it. Don Miguel Luiz, in his wonderful book, "The Four Agreements" writes, *"Be impeccable in your word."* This means to keep your promises, no matter what. If you find yourself promising your life away to your teenaged children, then you need to set limits with yourself. This will eliminate a host of letdowns, disappointments and conflicts.

Have you ever responded to a request by your teen with *"We'll see . . ."* Many teenagers hear this nearly every day from one parent or the other. *"We'll see. . ."* puts your teen into a void, a demilitarized zone, so to speak where there is no solution to their dilemma and there is no answer to their question. They can't feel secure about the future. In the lives of teenagers, situations like this party are considered to be urgent and important. They need an immediate and concrete response, even if it displeases them.

Trust your gut and make the decision.

Your child interprets a *"we'll see. . ."* as *"no you can't"* and immediately they begin their counter-attack in an effort to get you to change your mind. This tactic usually backfires because even though you are considering the possibility, your teen may become so annoying that you have no choice but to tell them "No."

However, if their efforts succeed in getting a yes out of you, then it's worth their time and energy. They learn that they can pressure you into acquiescing to their will. The primary problem with the *"we'll see. . ."* is it doesn't satisfy anybody's needs. They need to know your answer NOW and if you deny them, they will demand to know why you are denying them. Then you need them to stop bugging you and go away. Far too many parent-teen conflicts begin with *"we'll see. . ."* It's more effective to give them your answer as soon as possible. Like in the example above, there is no argument. They have a prior commitment. Don't worry about what your spouse or partner will think. You're here now. You're in charge and you need to make the decision. Be honest with your teen. If the answer is no, then explain your reasoning.

I know you have memories of trying to coerce or manipulate your parents into changing their minds. Go ahead and tell your teen one of these stories to remind them that what they are doing is as old as time. Whether or not your efforts were successful, let your teen know that you've been there and you are committed to doing a better job of parenting than your parents. You have learned from their mistakes and even though your teen may not appreciate it today, they will down the road.

Handy Insight

Teenagers do what it takes to <u>do</u> what <u>they</u> want to do. They also do what it takes <u>not</u> to do what <u>you</u> want them to do. Don't worry about this. They are practicing the negotiating skills needed to succeed out there in the world. Go ahead, barter with them.

With *Two Little Words* there is no need for arguing, yelling, screaming or any drama. When you hold yourself and your kids accountable for thoughts, feelings, and actions, you are building a solid foundation for your relationship over the long haul. Integrity is the foundation that all healthy relationships are built upon.

Until now I've been talking about how the boy in the example felt, but what did his parents feel? His parents may have been *startled* initially as they heard their child struggling with the door and then nearly tripping over the dog as he rushed in. I'm certain they felt *surprised* (when their son asked to go to a party instead of spending time with the family, as planned.) These parents might also have felt *irritation and frustration* (over their son's desire to bail on his commitment), *confusion* (from having to reconsider the evening's plans), *disappointment* (at their son's prioritizing his friends over the family), and *satisfaction* (over having stuck to their guns).

Everyone in this scenario is feeling a variety of mixed and powerful emotions. These emotions can be overwhelming and are a main reason conflict arises between parents and teenagers. It is critical that you manage your emotional responses to these sudden and I might add urgent changes in your teenager's priorities. Knee jerk and contradictory behaviors are normal for adolescents. They are expanding their world from a family based world to a peer based world. Don't let their chaos intrude upon your peace and tranquility.

Two Little Words also offers parents an easy-to-use tool that calms the stormy seas of adolescence. It teaches your kids the value of following through with commitments, even when there may be more enticing things to do. Nobody likes to miss a special event because of a prior commitment but if you are going to be a person of your word, this is what it takes. Everyone has to let go of disappointment when you have a choice between a previous commitment and a much more attractive alternative.

Use *Two Little Words* often and eventually your teenager will be able to tell their friends they have a prior commitment. They will even be able to say to their friend they hate to miss the party, but they are hanging out with the family that night. They become a person of honor and integrity.

Two Little Words also comes in handy for daily chores around the house as well as homework. These are two activities that your son or daughter will naturally put off. How many times have you heard *"I'll do it later"*? This is a normal adolescent response to what they view as intrusiveness on your part.

When you look back, ask yourself how many times did you say *"I'll do it later"* to your parents? These situations are perfect for using *Two Little Words*. As you know, your kids are busy people and they can't be bothered with such trivial things like homework and chores. After all, why should they be bothered by such drudgery? Can't you see how busy they are? They have friends to talk to. They have television to watch. There's the mall to go to and they have to eat and sleep as well.

Fun Facts about Adolescents

In Positive Discipline for Single Parents authors, Jane Nelsen, Cheryl Erwin, and Carol Delzer make this point: "It is always the relationship that matters most. Tips and techniques are great, but what matters most is a relationship between parent and child that is based on unconditional love and trust. If that relationship is strong – if your children know beyond a shadow of a doubt that you love them no matter what – you can make a lot of mistakes and still come out okay. All parenting skills and ideas work best when they're based on a foundation of love. Techniques without love are just that: techniques. Taking the time to build the proper foundation through words and actions, by talking, laughing, playing, and just being together, may be the best investment you make in your children."

I have discovered a powerful corollary to *Two Little Words.* I call it . . . .

"No Fun 'Til Done" or NFTD

When NFTD is implemented, you may get a similar response as with the party scenario. There may be mumbling and grumbling if not outright rebellion when you say,

"Nevertheless, your homework needs to be completed before you watch TV."

or

"Regardless of wanting to chat with your friends online, you need to take care of your chores first."

When parents are consistent in applying the NFTD strategy, they help their son or daughter improve their ability to take care of business by deferring gratification until the stupid, repulsive, idiotic and dumb homework or chore is completed. When your son or daughter learns this lesson, they become a much more reliable person. In addition, they feel much better about themselves and their ability to get things done. Doesn't it feel good to complete a chore that you've been avoiding?

Consistency is the key to super sizing NFTD. The more consistently you set limits with your teen, the easier it becomes and the more likely your teen will increase their ability to respond or response-ability. The better they become at following through on a promise, the more successful they will be as adults. At first, this may not be easy, especially if you are in the habit of allowing your son or daughter to put things off. By the way, if they see you putting things off then it will be impossible to use NFTD effectively.

You can expect a certain amount of resistance on their part. Their priorities are different than yours. Their priority is to do what they want to do when they want to do it. Don't let this make you crazy and don't take it personal. But, do hold them accountable.

How many times have you asked your teen about a school project that is coming due and they respond with,

"Oh, I've got plenty of time to do that."
or
"I'll do it right after I get off the phone."

OK, that sounds reasonable until you see them two hours later, still on the phone. At that point many parents become angry with their child. This does no good at all. Anger never teaches or reaches anyone. Yes, you may gain compliance by using anger in these situations, but is that what you really want? There is a lot of fallout when anger is used to manipulate your teens into taking care of business. Using NFTD is much more effective than anger when working with a procrastinating teen.

Ask yourself this question, *"Do I want their obedience or do I want their cooperation?"* As a parent, you have the power to get your teen's obedience because you have power and control over their lives, but is this really what you want? The time and energy it takes to get your teen to *"obey"* can be better spent developing an atmosphere of cooperation. Yes, you can probably get your teen to obey (for a while), but there are casualties from an authoritarian style of parenting. One casualty is the quality of the relationship you have with them. By soliciting cooperation you create a win-win situation where your need and your kid's need are met, simultaneously.

As you approach your highly socialized teen all you need to do is remind them that there is no problem if they want to talk with their friends, but first there is work to be done and when they are finished with their school project, they can talk all they want with their friends. Don't be surprised if they take a parting shot at you as they hang the phone up. That's OK. Let them have the last word. Their frustration and anger is not about you, but it may be the only way they have to regain a sense of power and control over their lives. No matter what do not let your teen provoke you into becoming angry, it only gives them an excuse to continue to procrastinate or perhaps outright refuse to do anything. In these conflicts your teen becomes focused on how unreasonable and unfair you are instead of focusing on their project or chore.

When your teen finally takes action and begins that school project or chore it is a good idea to use *The Hit and Run* to acknowledge them (See Chapter 2). To do this, go to where they are feverishly working on the project or chore and quietly say,

"I'm so glad to see you taking care of business, I am very proud of you."

Remember to leave immediately and give them some time and space for your acknowledgment to sink in. By doing so, you reinforce the behavior you want AND the behavior they need in order to succeed. Keep this intervention short, sweet and simple. Do not expect any gratitude from them. If they do come back and thank you for your support, simply look at them, smile and say, *"It's my pleasure."*

Handy Insight

It does not matter how carefully you choose your words or how calm you are. To your teenager it is unreasonable that you expect them to do schoolwork when it is <u>obvious</u> that they would rather be talking with their friends. Do not take this personally. They are simply practicing the art of controlling their lives.

As you have seen in this chapter, *Two Little Words* is a very effective way of setting limits and maintaining those limits with your teen. This tip will save you time and energy. In addition, how many conflicts and power struggles in the past could have been prevented if you had been familiar with the power of these *Two Little Words,* nevertheless and regardless?

Ten Tips to Tame Your Teen

Chapter 4

Shields Up Scotty

*"Children today are tyrants. They contradict
their parents, gobble their food, and tyrannize
their teachers." ~ Socrates*

At times, everyone is vulnerable to the
slings and arrows that are flung by people close
to them. You, like many parents of teenagers,
may feel like this is the rule rather than the
exception. In fact, all parents of adolescents
have been bombarded, assaulted, attacked,
belittled, disrespected or insulted by their teens.
Do not take this personally and engage your
shields. *Shields Up Scotty* creates an emotional
space that protects you from the emotional
fallout from your teenager. You know how
much emotional fallout teenagers have, but did
you know that you have a protective shield at
your disposal anytime you need it.

Without *Shields Up Scotty,* you are at
risk to misinterpret your teens intent. Without
Shields Up Scotty you might take your teen's
words and actions personally. Without *Shields
Up Scotty* you might have one or two less
children. I know it's frustrating when your
teen's behavior crosses the line and besides the
shock, you may also feel hurt, rejected, dejected
and maybe even threatened. If you are caught

off guard and feeling this way your most likely response is to get angry.

I know at times, when your feelings are hurt you fight fire with fire; that is, you become angry with your teen. If this happens frequently in your family, then you really need *Shields Up Scotty*. Raising your shields is a powerful neutralizing tool and deflects the negative energy that is flying around your teen. Just because life sucks for them is no reason for you to get angry. Besides, it's your job to be the grownup in these situations. Being grown up means no yelling, no screaming, no hollering, no throwing things and most importantly, no killing!

Shields Up Scotty, helps you to <u>detach</u>, emotionally from what is going on around you. With your shields up, there is no sense of urgency even though your teen may be demanding an immediate response. With your shields up, you feel calm, assured, and you are patient with your teenager. You <u>know</u> deep down that they need you to be patient and understanding at this time. At that moment they need you to be steady and strong. They need to trust that you can help them solve the problem at hand.

But, parents are not always calm, cool and collected. Most parents report that they are really stressed out! Throw teenagers into the mix and who knows what can happen. Many, if not most parents are tired, overworked, overwhelmed and worried about their kids. When you mix powerful emotions like these with adolescents, you get a time bomb that can explode at any moment. When you respond to your angry teen with anger it only makes more anger. Anger only escalates the conflict. Instead of having one person going crazy, i.e. your teen; you now have two or three people going crazy.

Handy Insight

Emotions are energy and they attract similar emotions. Anger attracts anger, anxiety attracts anxiety, joy attracts joy and love attracts love.

Getting angry with your teen is like pouring gasoline onto a fire, and thinking it will put it out. All parents become angry with their children. In fact, anger is so common in families that most people believe it is normal and healthy. Anger is never normal, rarely healthy and it is never a helpful response to your teen. This is why you need to know how to use *Shields Up Scotty,* and when to use it. When you engage your shields, you activate an "energy field" that blocks the negative energy your teen is directing at you. You are the adult and you know that conflict cannot be resolved if both parties are angry. Conflict cannot be resolved even if one person is angry. Anger only causes problems and never solves them. This is the time to love your child, regardless of how unlovable they are at the moment.

Shields Up Scotty can be engaged any time your son or daughter is angry. When you activate your shields, you give yourself a different perspective and with this new way of seeing things you recognize who owns the problem. Many parents get sucked into solving a problem that was not theirs to begin with. By using *Shields Up Scotty*, you can step back, take a few deep breaths, regain your composure and see the problem more clearly. Unless there is imminent danger do not try to stop your teen from doing what they are doing. It's not your job to control your teen; it's their job. Let me repeat that.

It is not <u>your</u> job to control your teen. It is <u>their</u> job!

Besides, how can you teach your kids to respond to difficult situations calmly if you're running around ranting like a madman? Calm energy attracts calm energy. Be calm and your teen will calm down.

There's nothing you can do to prevent your son or daughter from becoming angry with you and there is no way to predict when such an event will occur. There is one thing you <u>can</u> do which will have the greatest impact. Do this and eventually things will calm down. *You can do nothing!*

That's right, <u>do nothing</u>. Well, almost nothing. Engage your shields and maintain your composure. When you feel calm and emotionally detached, then, and only then, will you be able see that this problem is not yours; it's your teenager's problem. Eureka! Knowing who owns the problem is the first step to resolving it. You're not the one who is upset. You're not the one who is angry and you are not the one who is yelling and cursing. Therefore, it must be their problem. No matter what, <u>do not fight fire with fire</u>. Do not get caught up in their drama. *Shields Up Scotty* helps you to be a calming force when your teen is anything but calm.

With *Shields Up Scotty* fully engaged you have a clearer perspective and you are more objective, therefore more able to respond to your teen in a helpful way. Do not solve the problem for them, but encourage them to use their own resources.

Keep in mind that helping does not mean doing it for them. You know the old adage:

"Give a man a fish and you feed him for a day. Teach a man to fish and you feed him for a lifetime."

Every problem your teen has is an opportunity to learn how to fish. *Shields Up Scotty* helps you to stay calm and be objective while, at the same time supporting your teen's resourcefulness, resolve, and commitment to solving the problem, their way. Here is a simple suggestion on how to engage *Shields Up Scotty*.

If your teenager is in your face and I mean <u>in your face</u>, the first thing to do is take one step backwards, literally. When your teen is angry, it is critical to have physical space between you (at least an arm's length). By increasing the physical space you get a new perspective that helps you to be there for your teen in the most meaningful way possible. Stepping back not only gets your space back, it gives you an opportunity to assess how you are feeling at that moment. Be particularly alert to any sensation of irritation, agitation, frustration, hurt, anxiety, fear, resentment, or anger. These emotions are your body's natural response to a perceived threat. It is critical that you do not respond to these very powerful feelings. <u>Notice these emotions, but do nothing</u>.

Now that your shields are up take several deep, slow breaths and say to yourself, *"This is not my problem, it's her problem."* Repeat this phrase while you breathe slowly and deeply. Close your eyes if it helps to calm yourself. The purpose for *Shields Up Scotty* is to get back to your true loving self before you respond to your teens sense of urgency. Your teen may not believe it, but most everything can wait a moment or two. After several breaths and several rounds of saying your calming mantra, you will return to that peaceful, easy feeling. If you are still agitated, then keep your shields up until you feel calm and are certain that you will remain calm.

Fun Facts about Adolescents

Dr Sarah-Jayne Blakemore of the University College London Institute of Cognitive Neuroscience has found from brain scans that when compared to adults, kids from age 8 through the teen years use less of an area of the brain involved in empathy and emotional evaluation when making decisions about the reactions of themselves and others to future hypothetical situations. In other words according to the UCLA neuroscientist, teenagers take less account than adults of people's feelings and, often, even fail to think about their own. The results, presented at the BA Festival of Science, show that teenagers hardly use the area of the brain that is involved in thinking about other people's emotions and thoughts, when considering a course of action."

All adolescents test limits. It's their job to expand and explore their potential. Limit testing is part of the process of defining who they are and what they are capable of. *Shields Up Scotty* helps you to maintain your calm at times when you may otherwise lose control. By protecting your buttons and remaining calm, you improve your ability to think clearly AND you model for your teen how to handle difficult and emotionally charged situations. *Shields Up Scotty* is not an exercise in *"biting your tongue"*

or *"waiting to get in your 2-cents worth."* *Shields Up Scotty* allows you to observe and assess the situation with little to no attachment. With your shields up, you can be in the moment at the moment. *Shields Up Scotty* helps you to practice what I call Zen Parenting. If you invest your emotions in stopping the outburst, controlling the situation or changing your teen's behavior then you are not using this tip correctly. Remember, it is not your job to control their behavior, it's their job. *Shields Up Scotty* simply creates a boundary where you become aware of who has the problem, you or your teen.

Obviously if your son or daughter is angry or distraught, as parents you have a natural urge to take action to get the situation under control or get your child under control. DON'T DO IT! This is NOT your problem! Stay calm and be patient while silently observing the drama unfolding in front of you. Think about it, when you are upset and angry how open are you to someone telling you to calm down?

How does your teen appear to be doing? How are you doing? Take some more deep breaths but don't say anything. I know you have a lot to say about what is happening, but remember, you're *Brain Damaged*. Continue to be patient and wait. Your teen will eventually calm down and if they are open to some affection, then by all means touch them or give them a hug. At this point you can reassure and let them know that you love them and will always be there for them, even if you can't be perfect all the time.

When your teenager is calm, it is time for a gentle and sincere, *"Now, what's going on?"* Let them talk while you listen. When you are patient you learn about things that your teenager has been withholding (in an effort to be more grown up). You can say to them,

"Wow, you were really angry! What's going on?"

or

"What just happened here tells me that you may be under a lot of pressure. What's going on?

You may learn that they have been under tremendous pressure trying to be perfect. Now is the time to validate their experience and their emotions. <u>Do not judge them.</u>

When teenagers feel pressured it often causes them to overreact to ordinary events. For example, your daughter might burst into tears and suddenly leave the dinner table, when asked how her day at school was. Or your son may suddenly become sullen and withdrawn when you ask him how band practice went. These reactions have nothing to do with you or the questions you asked. <u>They are reacting to a part of themselves that believes they are inadequate in some way.</u>

Handy Insight
Frustration is your body's way of telling you to practice being patient.

When you are calm and practicing patience you are going to be more productive.

<u>Remember, you are the adult and your teenager needs you to be more grown up than they are.</u> Besides, your teen is only doing what she or he knows to do. Teach them to be patient by being patient with them. Like emotions attract like emotions. Patience attracts patience.

Your response to your teen's emotionality may be a habit you learned from your parents, a reaction they had when you were a teen. Parents oftentimes are <u>reacting</u> to their adolescent instead of <u>responding</u> to them. Have you ever heard your mother or father's voice come out of your mouth? When this occurs then you're reacting and not responding. When you are reacting to events around you, you are not being <u>response-able</u>. As a good enough parent, you want your teen to do well in school, make good decisions, and succeed in their chosen careers. You want your children to grow up to be responsible adults, right?

John Bradshaw, author of *Bradshaw on the Family* looks at responsibility in this way. He states, *"responsibility"* is *"the ability to respond."* In Bradshaw's perspective, your ability to respond appropriately to any given situation defines how responsible you are. Your ability to respond is directly linked to your ability to use critical thinking to determine the most appropriate response at any given time.

When you stop reacting to your teen and start responding, amazing changes take place in the nature and quality of your relationship. Your relationship with your teenager is critical for their success and believe it or not your relationship <u>is</u> at risk during this turbulent time.

Activating your shields takes practice. Stop yourself from taking control when your teen is out of control. Don't waste time and energy trying to get your son or daughter to calm down. Activate your shields as soon as you start to feel frustrated or angry and start breathing slowly and deeply to let go of these emotions. The problem is not yours to solve, it is your teen's problem to solve.

Handy Insight

Never use the word "tantrum" when your teen is upset. It's like throwing gasoline on a fire.

Take several deep breaths and say to yourself, *"Now stay calm, it's not my problem."* Keep repeating this mantra while taking deep breaths until you are calm and can <u>observe</u> the "tantrum" without feeling the urge to strangle them. By waiting and listening, you allow your teen to burn off the energy that is driving their behavior. Keep your shields up until the storm has passed and the coast is clear. The key to super- sizing *Shields Up, Scotty* is to be calm and emotionally detached from what you see and hear going on.

Fun Facts about Adolescents

In the article, Understanding Adolescent Emotional Development which was adapted from Walt Mueller, it states, "Remain sensitive. The variety of emotions that teens experience is very real to them. Many stem from a preoccupation with self and the accompanying fear of rejection. Teens expect their parents will always love and accept them. To be written-off by an insensitive parent is the type of rejection that can send a "normal" teen over the edge to clinical depression and even suicide. What teens need are parents who will hang in there and love them in spite of the load of emotional ups and down over what may seem to be trivial things. It may appear our kids are overreacting. But to them, they are handling the confusion in the best way they know how. Listen with sensitivity as they share their joys and fears.

How Guilt and Shame Impact Adolescent Development

Teenagers are <u>filled</u> with guilt and shame. Even if they don't act guilty, they feel this emotion almost daily. Guilt and shame are not the same thing and it is important to distinguish the two of them. Here's a simple way to tell them apart.

- Guilt tells us we MADE a mistake

- Shame tells us we ARE the mistake.

- Guilt compels us to TALK about the problem and make amends.

- Shame compels us to HIDE the problem and avoid talking about it.

If your teenager feels a lot of shame, then they believe something is wrong with them. Unlike guilt, shame shuts you down and closes the door to communication. Shame stifles you, and makes you feel small and insignificant.

There are many ways that parents unknowingly contribute to their teen's feelings of shame. I know you don't want to cause your kid to feel ashamed, but it is nearly impossible to avoid. Kids who feel a lot of shame will distort your words and actions to be negative and therefore, proof of their inadequacy. It's important to be aware of the messages you are sending with your words and your deeds. Everyone knows what it is like to have another person belittle, embarrass, make fun of, ridicule, demean or discourage them. You may not know this, but your kids encounter this nearly every day. They need you to be there for them. They need you to listen.

Did you know that focusing on how smart, pretty, cute, beautiful, handsomest, greatest or best can also cause your teen to feel worse about themselves? Your smart and handsome teen may not feel the same way you do about them. Pay attention and notice how your teen reacts to compliments. If they downplay, minimize or deny the compliment, it may not be modesty. It may be a sign they don't feel good about themselves. Because the world can be a vicious place they need you to see them as capable and competent. It is important to be encouraging, not discouraging.

Yes, even though your teen thinks you are *Brain Damaged*, your opinion is still important. Whether you believe it or not, they do pay attention to what you think and say about them. Even if he screams, *"I don't care what you think."* He does care. She may look all grown up, but emotionally and financially she is still dependent upon you. The stronger their self-esteem and self-image is, the easier it is for them to take the risks necessary to become an independent, self-sufficient and happy adult. The weaker their self-esteem, the more difficult life becomes.

Handy Insight

The amount of Anger (A) your teen acts out is equal to the amount of Vulnerability (V) they feel. The formula: A = V is always true.

Teenagers who feel a lot of shame express a lot of anger. Ironically, anger is the perfect antidote to shame. Shame makes you feel weak and vulnerable while anger makes you feel strong and powerful. People with a lot of shame, frequently act out with anger. This is why it is important for parents to identify the underlying causes of their teen's angry outbursts and not focus solely on the angry behavior. Look beneath the surface when your adolescent gives you a $10 response for a $1 problem. If you AND your teen become angry with each other, you run the risk of becoming locked into what I call a *Nuclear Chain Reaction or NCR*.

The *Nuclear Chain Reaction* is an escalating series of reactions between two people where the action of one is the stimulus for the reaction of the other. In other words, if you react angrily to something your teen has said or done and they respond angrily to you, a *Nuclear Chain Reaction* has just been triggered. The first person reacts to an event, then the second person reacts to the reaction of the first person, then the first person reacts to the reaction of the second person. In no time at all, the original problem has been forgotten. This *"reacting to reactions"* continues, fueling itself until the bomb explodes <u>or</u> one of you chooses not to be fuel. As the adult, it is your job to <u>not be</u> fuel because your teen can <u>only</u> be fuel at times like this. The *Nuclear Chain Reaction* is very destructive to all relationships, but in families with teenagers it is devastating. The more NCR's that occur in your family the more damage you and those you love are experiencing. *Nuclear Chain Reactions* do not occur in healthy relationships.

Please take a moment and think about a time when you were in a power struggle or NCR with your teenaged son or daughter. Ask yourself the following questions as you remember that event and identify the signs of a *Nuclear Chain Reaction*.

- How did the conflict start?

- What was the conflict about originally?

- What did you end up arguing about?

- What did you do to "add fuel?"

- How did your teen add fuel?

- What were you feeling during the power struggle, other than anger?

- What do you imagine your teenager was feeling other than anger?

- How did the NCR end? Or did it?

It is important to resolve conflict as soon as possible. If left unchecked, a teeny weenie, itsy bitsy disagreement or misunderstanding can shift into a power struggle and before you know it you have a full scale *Nuclear Chain Reaction* on your hands. This is why *Shields Up Scotty* is such an important tip for parents of teenagers. This tip is your parachute when your parental plane is crashing. It can save the life of your relationship with your teen.

The sooner you recognize NCR's the sooner you can initiate *Shields Up Scotty.* Once your shields are up, say nothing and wait. While you are waiting, take several long, slow, deep breaths. Now that your shields are up, bring your attention to the moment. What's going on right now? Make a quick assessment of your emotional state and when you feel calm, ask your son or daughter, *"How are you feeling right now?"* <u>Asking this question is one of the most powerful things you can do.</u>

By shifting the focus from behaviors to emotions, you alter the nature of the conflict from defending to expressing. When authentic emotions are expressed, conflict is resolved. There is no guarantee that your teen will suddenly spill the beans, but you will certainly cause them to re-think what they are doing and why they are doing it. This also tells them you are concerned with how they feel.

The key to deactivating a *Nuclear Chain Reaction* is to not be fuel! Stop the NCR in its tracks by making a choice not to argue and add more fuel. As soon as you recognize the NCR, engage your shields, take 3 deep, slow breaths, open up your peripheral vision and step back (physically) if necessary. By not adding fuel to the fire, the only energy left is the energy coming from your teen. Calmly allow them to burn this extra fuel off. In a moment or two they will be calm and ready to talk. If neither of you are ready to talk, that's alright too. Utilize *The Hit and Run* to gracefully exit the scene until at which time both of you are calm.

Nuclear Chain Reactions happen very quickly and often lead to dangerous if not abusive situations in the family. Do not let yourself get caught up with this highly destructive dynamic. Take control of your emotional state; even if it means leaving the room. Nothing good can happen if you try to get to the bottom of an NCR before all of the fuel has been burned off. It is very easy to trigger another episode by trying to resolve the problem before all parties are ready to discuss it. When everyone is ready, besides the obvious problem, it is important to talk about how the situation got out of control so quickly. Understanding your personal family dynamics will greatly reduce the number of NCRs that occur.

Handy Insight
Reduce NCRs significantly by talking with each other about how things spun out of control.

Now take a moment and practice putting your shields up and bringing them down. Pay particular attention to what it feels like when your shields are up versus when they are down. Practice *Shield's Up Scotty* throughout the day. Use this tip when you feel stressed, overwhelmed, pressured, at your wits end, or think you're going crazy. These are wonderful times to put your shields up. Pay attention to even the slightest hint of discomfort and engage your shields. Nobody needs to know you are doing this and as you breathe in deeply and slowly, put a small smile on your face, you know, a look of contentment.

There are two reasons why you cannot avoid *Nuclear Chain Reactions*.

1) Nuclear Chain Reactions are unavoidable.

2) Avoiding a possible NCR increases the likelihood it will occur.

The *Nuclear Chain Reaction* is responsible for ending most relationships. That's right. If there are chronic and unresolved NCR's in any relationship, it will destroy the communication and trust to the point where neither of you can stand being in the same room. Don't let this happen to your family! Learn to recognize NCR's when they are young and disengage.

The problem is never <u>what</u> is going on around you, but how you <u>respond</u> to what is going on. Make it a priority to use *Shields Up Scotty* every day, even if there is no reason to. The more you practice, the easier it will be to engage your shields. Soon, it will be as easy as flipping a switch to turn on the light.

As you can see, the *Nuclear Chain Reaction* is a slippery slope to nowhere. Notice how each person in the scenario above is reacting to the reaction of the other person. The issue of the homework is all but lost. Rather than putting energy into avoiding situations you cannot avoid in the first place, put your energy into recognizing an NCR the minute it begins. Be pro-active and disengage immediately from this very deadly pattern.

Shields Up Scotty is your first line of defense any time you are confronted with an angry adolescent. The shields you develop help you to respond to your teenager instead of reacting in a knee jerk fashion. Your teenager, however, <u>will continue to react</u> for of a couple of reasons.

1. They do not have the ability to remain calm and collected in difficult or stressful situations.

2. They lack experience and they have had little practice managing strong emotions.

Shields Up Scotty, effectively disarms the NCR by preventing you from adding fuel to the fire. Then, it's simply a matter of time until your teen's *extra fuel* is burned off and you can bring your shields down. But be prepared to engage your shields again at a moment's notice.

Start at the Bottom Left Box

NUCLEAR CHAIN REACTION®

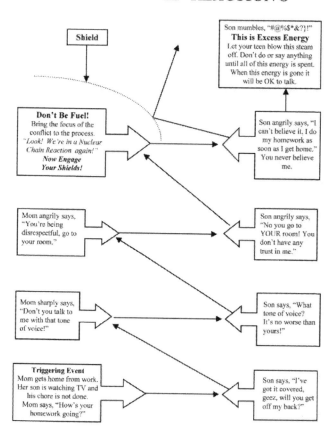

In the early 1990's I worked at a private psychiatric hospital in Sacramento, CA. After lunch one day I returned to the adolescent unit. As soon as I stepped onto the floor and the door slammed shut, I was confronted by an irate 15-year-old girl. She had been waiting for me and had a bone to pick. I'm pretty sure very few of you have been challenged by an angry 15-year-old girl in a psychiatric hospital. It is not a pretty sight. Parents who have had a child hospitalized in a "nut house" know how quickly events can escalate and become volatile.

Of course, at the time, I am caught by off guard, *ambushed* by this wild eyed teenager with a full head of steam and her sails full of wind. Her face was inches from mine. I mean she was literally <u>in my space and in my face</u>. As she glared into my eyes she said in as menacing a tone as she could muster, *"Ray, you told me you were going to call my parents and you didn't!"* I looked into her dark steely gaze and took one step backwards. By stepping back I not only regained my personal space, but I also gained a brief moment to gather myself. I activated *Shields Up Scotty* and took a deep breath, perhaps two or three. Then I looked her straight in the eye and said, *"You're right. I have not contacted your parents and I apologize for not getting to it sooner."* The wind in her sails disappeared completely and the steam stopped pouring out of her ears. Her entire demeanor shifted from being hurt and angry to understanding and acceptance that I too was doing the best I could.

She expected me to deny responsibility for the promise I had made and placate her with some trite comment, like *"Don't worry about it, I'll call them later."* She expected me to argue with her and to minimize her needs. *Shields Up Scotty* effectively eliminated a power struggle. Because no struggle occurred and I made it clear that her concerns were a priority, she was able to let go of her anger.

In this situation, I stepped back and engaged my shields to protect myself, but the one thing that made the difference was validating her truth. I made it clear, in no uncertain terms that she was correct. I had not called her parents. I validated her reality in an undeniable way. By acknowledging her she was able to let go of her feelings of betrayal and be amenable to the realities of the situation. I assured her my priority that afternoon is to talk with her parents AND report back to her immediately following my conversation with them.

In the end there were many positive changes that occurred for that young woman and she was soon released from the hospital. Of course significant changes needed to occur within her family. I was able to help them understand what had happened and how to respond better to their child's needs. Without her parent's commitment there would not have been the dramatic improvements we witnessed. I tell you this story to illustrate the power of *Shields Up Scotty*. If it can help me be successful with an adolescent hospitalized for a psychiatric condition then you too can be successful. *Shields Up Scotty* will protect you at those times when your teen appears to be losing their mind. When *Shields Up Scotty* is used every day there are many happy endings, even in a psychiatric hospital.

Another reason the actions I took were so effective is because I combined two of the Ten Tips. When I stepped backwards and engaged my shields, I used *Shields Up, Scotty*. Once my shields were engaged and I was calm, cool and collected, I applied the second tip called *The Judo Approach*. I discuss this tip at length in the next chapter. Combining two or more tips is an easy way to increase the power of your response. Are you ready? Then put your *Shields Up, Scotty*.

Ten Tips to Tame Your Teen

Chapter 5

The Natural

"The best substitute for experience is being sixteen." ~Raymond Duncan

Experience is the greatest teacher of all. Experience helps teenagers to learn how to think for themselves and solve problems on their own. You know they will make many mistakes along the way. When mistakes are made, don't forget to use your *teen's* brain to come up with *natural* and *logical* consequences for any rule violations or inappropriate behavior. That's right; let your teen decide what the consequence should be then exercise your right to veto any consequence that:

1) **is not logically or naturally linked to the behavior**

2) **cannot be applied immediately or**

3) **can't be done at all**

Be patient with your teen as they experience the consequences of their poor decisions. When you allow your teens to experience *The Natural* consequences of their choices they have an opportunity to learn from them. Everyone experiences natural consequences. A natural consequence of going to work every day is getting paid for the days you work. A natural consequence of spilling milk is you need to clean it up.

Natural consequences can be applied to every situation that your teen experiences. They get their homework done and they can do what they want. Getting to do what they want is a natural consequence of doing their homework.

The most powerful factor in your ability to make good decisions is something you can't quite put your finger on, but you can feel it in your body, in the pit of your stomach. There are many names for this inner wisdom. You may call it a *gut feeling* or your *intuition*. You may know it as the voice of reason or your inner guide.

I call it *"the part of me that knows."* This *sense of knowing* is something we all have and it is essential part of the critical thinking skills necessary for survival. All of you have experienced this exact feeling at the very moment a decision is required. You may not have noticed it, but your inner wisdom was there.

Throughout my life, when I've listened to the part of me that knows, I have always been steered in the right direction. When I allow my fears or even my rational brain to convince me that this *gut feeling* is wrong, I've regretted it. I am certain each of you have your own stories of second guessing yourself or talking yourself into something bad or out of something good.

Eventually you realized this *sense of knowing* is accurate and at those times when you based your decisions on it, the outcomes were positive. I'm also certain that when you overrode that *gut feeling* with rational and logical thinking, the results did not turn out so well.

Your ability to know what to do is greatly enhanced by listening carefully to that small voice within. Not the voice that constantly chatters at you, but that deep, soft, calm and wise voice. When your decision is based on a *gut feeling*, then your critical thinking will be pointed in the right direction. Your plan of action will be devoid of fears or worries because your intuitive self knows the correct path to take. You want to instill this type of self-awareness and sensitivity in your kids.

Their intuition is a foolproof guidance system that when activated will guide them throughout their lives. They will feel comfortable being *responsible* because they have *the ability to respond* to any situation at any given time. Isn't this what you want for your kids? Don't you want them to be able to make good decisions? Then, encourage them to look within for the answers to their dilemmas.

Intuition is a part of what makes using *The Natural* so powerful. By experiencing *The Natural* consequences of their actions, your teen learns how trust their intuition. By increasing their self-awareness, they develop a relationship with their intuitive self and therefore improve their decision making ability. Teenagers are hard wired to explore the world and they <u>will</u> take risks with or without your permission <u>and</u> with or without your awareness. When you equip your teens with this powerful and most accurate "compass" they will be able to take responsibility for themselves. You do want your kids to trust their own judgment and make good decisions, right?

Handy Insight

The Natural provides feedback from the world about the quality of your teen's decisions. This teaches them how the world works.

In my work with teenagers I notice that the majority of these teens understand the relationship between their intuition and the outcome of their decisions. They recognize their *gut feelings* but don't pay attention to them. When your teen makes decisions based upon their *intuition* they feel more in control over their lives.

The Natural provides a framework for the development of your teen's self-awareness. Self-awareness leads to a greater ability to think critically, which leads to more self-confidence and ultimately to your teens ability to take responsibility for their lives. When your teenager becomes *response-able*, then their success is guaranteed. Natural consequences are a part of everyday living and are the outcomes of the choices that you make. Natural consequences are not a judgment of who you are, nor do they take into account your present situation. They are the physical manifestation of the decisions you have made in your life. Any judgment over your decision comes from you, not the environment. All experiences therefore are lessons for you, for me, for your teen and for everyone else. Life teaches life.

Since adolescents primarily learn from experience, it is important to give them opportunities to interact with the world and the tools they need to succeed. Good enough parents realize that they can leverage the most powerful need adolescents have, the need for personal freedom. I realize this may not be news to you, but I am suggesting that you capitalize on this adolescent Holy Grail, their desire to be autonomous and free. This is a win-win situation that has enormous value. Below is a simple formula to guide you.

$$PR = AF$$

Where:
PR = personal responsibility
and
AF = amount of freedom

In other words:
Personal Responsibility = Amount of Freedom

Because society expects you to be responsible for teaching your kids everything they need to know to live on their own, I came up with this formula to help you to be more effective at this huge responsibility.

This formula simply states, *"The Amount of Freedom that your adolescent receives is in direct proportion to the amount of Personal Responsibility they take on."* The amount of responsibility and freedom they assume will depend upon your individual beliefs and values, not mine. This is where you and your teenager need to negotiate and identify concrete examples of how they can increase their personal freedom through increased responsible behavior. Every family will look at this task differently, but regardless of the individual differences and the infinite possibilities, the formula still holds true. As personal responsibility increases so does the amount of freedom your teenager earns. This is true for everyone.

This is an important relationship for teenagers to understand. When adults take on increased levels of personal responsibilities there is an equivalent increase in personal freedom. By taking care of your responsibilities to your employer, you get a paycheck and with this money you have more choices and you can more freely express yourself. Naturally, on the other, hand if you neglect your responsibilities to your employer you may soon lose your job thereby decreasing your choices and your ability to express yourself freely.

By applying *PR = AF* you help your adolescent learn how to prioritize. Has your teen ever asked for permission to go to a friend's house when you know their homework is not done and they have not taken out the garbage? Although going to a friend's house is not a problem, your concern is that they have not taken care of business. When you allow your child to go to their friend's house without taking care of business you give them the message that one obtains their freedom before they become responsible. Do you get paid before you go to work? Of course not! By applying *The Natural*, you can easily support your teen's desire to see a friend *and* support their need to take care of business.

Using *The Natural* means that homework and chores have priority over going to a friend's house. If your teen is not taking care of responsibilities, *The Natural* consequence is a decrease in their freedom. Your son or daughter is not likely to embrace these priorities with enthusiasm, but learning to take care of business first is a most valuable lesson. Over time, by carefully applying PR = AF and using *The Natural*, you soon discover that the young adult in your household is behaving more responsibly. They may even surprise you by doing their homework and taking out the garbage before they ask to go to their friend's. Yes, it's really possible!

Amazing things happen when you use *The Natural* consistently to address your teen's forgetfulness, errors in judgment, impulsivity or any other painful dilemma they find themselves in.

I'm sure you have noticed that for your teen, everything is *urgent* and *important,* especially when it comes to their friends, but not so *urgent* and *important* when it comes to homework or chores. This attitude has nothing to do with their relationship with you; teenagers simply tend to put the cart before the horse. Don't you wish you had a dollar for every time your kid said, *"I'll do it later,"* referring to anything that they don't want to do now? So what is *The Natural* consequence for *"doing it later?"* It is a decrease in personal freedom. Remember NFTD, or "No Fun 'Til Done?"

NFTD helps you to avoid a power struggle. It keeps you from jumping in and pressuring your adolescent to do their chore on your time schedule.

Even if you win and the chore gets done, there is so much animosity between the two of you, that their work will be half-hearted, poorly done and everyone will become frustrated. When this occurs you may be compelled to tell your kid what a lousy job they have done. How is this helpful? This only creates more resentment and makes it more difficult the next time you need your kid to be helpful around the house.

Handy Insight

Would you rather have your teen's obedience or their cooperation? Think about it.

There are literally thousands of possible problems that can occur in day-to-day life. How can you know which consequence is the right one? The table on the next page provides a guideline to help you determine which consequence is the best match for your teen's errant behavior. You don't have to know. Use your teen's brain to come up with the consequence. If it meets the qualifications mentioned at the beginning of this chapter, then go with it.

Use this table to help you determine if their idea makes any sense. Then all you have to do is OK it or veto it. If it doesn't meet the standards mentioned on page 77, then veto it and send them back to the drawing board. Eventually they will hit the nail on the head and come up with a perfect consequence that drives the point home and maintains your relationship. Not to mention your sanity.

Table of Consequences
A Guideline for Parents of Teens

Teen Behavior	Real World Reference	Consequence
Homework Not Done	Work	No Fun Until It's Done
School Attendance	Work/Social	Limit Social Contacts
Not Doing Chores	Work	No Fun Until It's Done
Arguing	Social	Time Alone/Self Reflection
Picking On Siblings	Social	Time Alone/Self Reflection
Isolating In Room	Social	Engage In Family Activity
Messy Room	Personal	Chaos-Close the Door
Trouble Waking Up	Personal	Go To Bed Earlier
Tardiness At School	Work/Social	Limit Social Contacts
Hygiene	Personal/Social/ Work	Time Alone/Self-Reflection

Don't worry too much about assigning natural consequences for every little thing your child does or doesn't do. The problem is not in identifying natural consequences; it's in the letting go of outdated and entrenched parenting beliefs and behavioral patterns that have been with you since childhood.

Many of you have promised yourself never to treat your kids the way your parents treated you, however these old patterns are deeply imbedded and they affect the way you see the world and your role as a parent. These old and outdated habits come out when you are tired, hungry, anxious, hurt, frustrated, etc. Whether or not you want to admit it, there have been times when you reacted to your teen exactly like your mother or father. You may have even heard your parent's voice coming out of your mouth. This usually occurs in the midst of a *Nuclear Chain Reaction*. Even though this happens quite often in families it does not mean it's helpful. If you can't think of anything to say or do, it is a good idea to *do and say nothing*. It is in these moments of parental angst that the worst characteristics of your mother or father can emerge, striking swiftly and without warning.

These demons have the potential to haunt you and your family for your entire life. The Ten Tips provide you with options and insights to eliminate these ghostly patterns.

When these apparitions occur, and I know they do, take a moment to breathe deeply and regroup. These self-imposed time outs give you a moment to discover what is really going on with you. This is a time for reflection, not projection.

Fun Facts about Adolescents

In his book, The Adolescent Brain: Reaching for Autonomy, Robert Sylwester has the following to say about natural consequences: "Young people will also learn how the natural and cultural worlds work in their 20-year development and that their behavior has natural consequences. For example, equipment broken by misuse does not operate; a stated unkind comment can't be deleted. But they'll also learn that adults will often inappropriately ascribe unrelated negative natural consequences to behavior. "If you don't clean up your room immediately, you can't watch TV this evening." Such comments simply confuse young people who correctly perceive no natural relationship between the organization (or disorganization) of their bedroom and watching TV in the living room. The natural consequence of Sylwester's example might be to remind the adolescent that all who share a home must help maintain the public and private areas. An adolescent who chooses to not maintain personal space (one's room) can thus be evicted from that space or be required to maintain a greater-than-equal share of the public space (such as the living room or the yard), but not participating in the maintenance of the home is not an option. Such adult rhetoric thus delays the development of a clear differentiation between natural and contrived consequences and so also the development of adult autonomy."

Sometimes the tension in the household is so thick; you can cut it with a knife. Humor can disarm these volatile moments. Admit that you are *Brain Damaged.* This can provide the levity and the energy needed to prevent the conflict from

developing into a *Nuclear Chain Reaction*
Examples of such statements are:

> *"I am flabbergasted and for the life of me, I
> have no idea what is going on right now. Look at
> what are we doing to each other?"*
>
> or
>
> *"Isn't this silly, here we are getting all worked up
> over nothing."*

Statements like this draw attention to the process and away from the object of contention, whether it their room, chores, homework, or relationships with peers and siblings. Once disarmed, the conflict can be resolved with minimal collateral damage.

You may hesitate at times to let *The Natural* consequences play themselves out. However, by suspending your fear of what *could* happen you will dramatically reduce the number of conflicts in your household <u>and</u> save incredible amounts of time and energy. Let your teen spend their time and energy. They have plenty of both.

For example, most parents want their children to do well in school and most children want to do well in school. In adolescence, academic performance can deteriorate in the wake of the physical, emotional, and social changes that occur. There are many reasons for this decline in performance and it is important to be aware of what you pay attention to. Be conscious of what you focus on. Are you more attentive to what you want or to what you don't want?

When you pay attention to a job well done, a pleasant conversation, or the enthusiasm and passion your teen expresses, this sends a message to them that they are important and you enjoy them. Possessed with the feelings that accompany this kind of parental admiration, they courageously take each step, one by one, into adulthood.

Fun Facts about Adolescents

In an article published on the internet by Parent Line, some principles for using natural consequences are outlined.

- *Consequences should always be logically connected to the behavior*

- *The parent can use a neutral, firm but kind tone of voice. There is no need to get upset as the consequences themselves will have an impact on the child.*

Consequences work best when they are used consistently. If there is a particular type of behavior which is often a problem, use the same consequence consistently. This will make it predictable for the child, so they will start to predict for themselves "what happens next if I do this..."

Discipline is just one aspect of your life with your teenager (although sometimes it can seem like 100 percent!) Try to develop the parts of your relationship that do work well, such as chatting together, having fun.

The most powerful consequences often come from the child themselves. Ask them what they think a reasonable consequence of their behavior should be, and negotiate it with them.

Teenagers as a group are very insecure. They need constant validation by their parents, teachers and peers. They need you to notice that they <u>can</u> do things well and they need to know they are a joy and pleasure for you as opposed to a burden or a worry. <u>Because teenagers are taking their first steps out into the world, they need to know they are loved and cared about at home.</u>

Build a repertoire of positive natural consequences that work for you and your teen. If they enjoy talking on the phone (and what teenager doesn't?) you can use this activity as a consequence for the help they give or for being kind to a younger sibling. Catch your teen in the act of being generous, kind, helpful, courteous, insightful, resourceful and creative; or for just being who they are. Zoom in and pay attention. Take your teen aside at those times and tell them how proud you are and how much you appreciate them. Using *The Natural* in positive ways will be ten times more powerful than any punishment you can dish out. In fact, forget about punishment altogether, let the world provide the consequences for your teen in the most natural way.

Handy Insight

Pay attention to what your teen does that
you appreciate and say something about it.
Water your plants and they will grow.

The Only Thing to Fear Is Fear Itself – Franklin Roosevelt

Let's talk about fear. Fear is the ego's playground. It's the culprit behind all of the problems in the world. Fear is a powerful communicator and it is a powerful tool. All governments know a fearful population is easily controlled. Some governments go so far as to induce fear through violence as a method of controlling the population. Fear is so powerful, that most of you don't want to talk about it. Many of you may have grown up in households where threats and punishments were the primary means of discipline and it was not safe to be afraid. Therefore, many you cannot admit it when you are afraid. If this is true for you, then your parents or caretakers had deeply rooted fears and they were acting out on those fears. They may have had more fear than love.

I have noticed a persistent pattern with parental fears, probably the same fears you are experiencing right now as your kid move into adolescence. This pattern has nothing to do with any specific fear, but is linked to the <u>intensity</u> of the fear. Worries and fears need to be minimized. Your worries and fears give your teen the message that you don't see them as competent and capable. They need your confidence until at which time they have enough of their own.

The more intense your worry or fears are, the less capable your teenager will feel and at some point they may give up trying to prove you wrong and go for proving you right. I have known many parents, whose greatest fear was their child will fail in school, not graduate and end up living a life of financial hardship and ruin. This is a really big fear, and you would be surprised to know how common it is among parents of adolescents. When fears this big and intense get triggered by a poor progress report then all hell breaks loose and the sky begins to fall. It's the end of the world for parents like this. What can their children do with this avalanche of anxiety?

When your fears are inflated it has the opposite effect on the desired behavior of your teenager. Parents who hold onto irrational fears, such as their child's imminent failure at school, tend to have children who fail at school.

Handy Insight
You get what you expect. So expect the best from your teen.

Some parents have fears so powerful and imbedded in their psyche that they cannot imagine anything but catastrophe happening. They are so familiar with this fear they call it normal worry. Deeply held adult fears are heavy loads for teenagers to carry. With all of these fears dominating the parent's life, there is little room for success. The progress report becomes an all or nothing event that places inordinate pressure on the teenager to perform for the parents benefit.

Naturally, the teen is unable to handle this emotional overload and oftentimes stops doing their best. Then the self-fulfilling prophecy occurs and that leads me to another formula. (Yes, I was a math teacher.)

$$PF = FC$$
Where:
PF = Parental Fear
and
FC = Fearful Child

In other words:
As parents become more fearful, so do their children.

If the fear is strong enough then a self-fulfilling prophecy occurs. <u>In the minds of fearful parents, the outcome justifies their fear and they strongly reject the possibility that their fear is creating the expected outcome.</u> This is a difficult shift in thinking for regular parents, but for the irrationally fearful parents, it is blasphemy and they defend their fears with detailed descriptions of a series of negative experiences that justify and solidify their beliefs.

The point is; irrational fear is counterproductive and destroys any possibility of your teen succeeding. These intense fears cause you to become overly involved in your adolescent's life and eventually you start blaming your teen for how your life is going. How can your kids take on responsibility for their own lives when they are saddled with responsibility for yours? I've worked with hundreds of young adults who don't believe in themselves as a result of having anxious and fearful parents. Don't let this happen to you and your family. Take full and complete responsibility for your feelings and for your life, then watch your teen take ownership for theirs.

Instead of holding onto fear and the resulting pessimism about your child's success, turn it around and cultivate an irrational *optimism* for your child's success. Be unflappably positive and optimistic about your teen's abilities and potential. Start right now and soon you will see positive changes in your child's behavior. By the way, you cannot fake optimism! You must be sincere. Your kids are too smart to fall for a half-hearted and dishonest attempt at optimism. You must truly feel confident in your teen's ability to succeed and be happy with their lives; even if there is very little evidence of that happening now. This may take some extra effort on your part, but it is well worth it. You may not immediately accept the notion that by changing your beliefs about your child, you can change their behavior, but you can. Try it!

When you make the shift from negative to positive, you pay more attention to what your child is doing right than to what your child is doing wrong. By focusing on their positive efforts you reinforce that behavior. When you pay attention to what your teen is doing wrong you reinforce that behavior. This is not rocket science. You get what you pay attention to.

Handy Insight
Positively reinforce positive behavior.

The most effective thing you can do is monitor yourself and become aware of what you are thinking and how you feel at any given moment. If you experience worry, that's alright, take some deep slow breaths and let it go.

However, if you find yourself paralyzed with fear, you need to identify the belief responsible for it and change that belief. Fear is a time bomb waiting to explode. Your child does not and cannot cause you to be anxious and fearful; they are merely triggers for your own deep seated fears. The bottom line is this; lighten up and so will your family.

The Dark Side of Natural Consequences

Employing *The Natural* is not necessarily the best course of action in every scenario. There are some downright dangerous and scary behaviors that teenagers do and if your teen is engaged in these behaviors then it requires strong and immediate action. You cannot compromise the safety of your children. As you know, there are plenty of dangers in the world to scare the pants off any well intended parent. But the scope of this book is not to address these very real and dangerous problems. There are plenty of books that can help you with that. This book was written to help you create a strong and mutually respectful relationship with your teenager. A strong parent-teen relationship is the best defense against the myriad of evils in the world.

Don't allow the media and all the crime and violence you see on television or read about take control of your good judgment. Look around and see for yourself. There are many more kind and loving acts going on in the world than negative acts. The vast majority of you have never been the victim of a violent crime. According to The Disaster Center only 0.5% of the US population has been a victim of a violent crime (murder, rape, robbery and assault). The percentage is higher for non-violent crime (burglary, larceny and auto theft), but at 3.33% does not by any means represent the average American's experience with crime. The media has created an image of our environment as dangerous, which obviously is not the case for the vast majority of you.

Most crime is concentrated in urban areas, which makes sense because of the population density. Those living in urban areas are more aware of the differences between real danger and perceived danger. Most parents living in cities take the necessary precautions to protect their children from crime and violence. In addition, crime is concentrated within the lower socio-economic neighborhoods of these urban centers.

What I'm saying is if you are fearful that you or a family member could be a victim of crime then you need to do something about it. Take some time to determine the facts related to crime and violence in your neighborhood. Form a neighborhood watch group. Be proactive in your response to the threat of crime and violence in your neighborhood. Taking action not only reduces your feelings of fear but actually reduces the incidence of crime and violence.

When you look at the statistics, many parental fears are unjustified. Letting go of this fear is not *"sticking your head in the sand"* it is contributing to the common good. I am discussing this issue in support of a positive and practical approach to dealing with your teen's exploits out in this big bad world. Remember the self-fulfilling prophecies discussed earlier in this chapter? Then let go of any irrational fear and if you can't eliminate it completely then reduce that fear to a simple worry. I trust your judgment and I believe in your common sense.

By doing this one thing for yourself you will be much less concerned about allowing *The Natural* consequences to play themselves out. Let go of fear and you open the door for your capable and competent teenager to learn what it takes to grow up. Always trust your kid's ability to overcome adversity even if it takes them several times to figure it out. Does the mighty oak ever doubt that the acorn will become a tree?

Handy Insight

Adolescents are so egocentric that virtually everything they do or don't do is in response to how they believe others perceive them.

So, what is clear and present danger in your child's world? That depends upon where you live and the quality of relationship between you and your teenager. The home is a much bigger influence than the street and most of the time there is more violence in the home than on the street. Teenagers with at-risk behavior are reacting to what's going on at home.

The lessons learned from experiencing *The Natural* consequences does not need to be super-sized, it already is super-sized. Trust your gut, trust your kid's ability, and let go of fear. Oh, and don't forget to breathe.

Ten Tips to Tame Your Teen

Chapter 6
What? Me Worry?

"The troubles of adolescence eventually all go away - it's just like a really long, bad cold." ~Dawn Ruelas

For most of you, concerns for the safety, security, and wellbeing of your children has been an all-consuming passion since the day your teen was born. However, letting go of this enormous responsibility is critical to ensure your teen's successful passage into adulthood. It may be scary being parents of an adolescent, but don't be afraid for them.

Your teen wants to get out there and be responsible for their life; they just don't know how to do it. This is where you come in. They need you to let go, just like you needed your parents to do when you were young. They *are* going to have problems and they *are* going to mess up in one way or another. It's inevitable and there is nothing you can do to prevent them from making these mistakes. That's the good news. Adolescence is a time when the world becomes their sparring partner. Worry all you want, but all it will do is create a gulf in your relationship with your teen. Growing up requires teenagers to do things they have never done before and making a mess of things is part of the process. If it were not for this turbulence, your teen would not learn how to solve problems. They wouldn't grow up and when they are 34 years old, they will be living at home and you will still be doing their laundry. If you don't want that to happen then get out of their way. *What? Me Worry?* helps you to let go and give your teen the responsibility for their life along with the privilege of solving any problems they create. Instead of generating solutions for your teen, *What? Me Worry?* encourages your teen to think for themselves. Statements like,

"Looks like you've got a problem there. What are you going to do about it?"

or

"What do you think is going to happen if you make that choice?"

help your teen to stay focused on problem solving their way. At first, these questions will likely irritate or annoy your teen. They are used to you solving problems for them and they will resist coming up with solutions of their own. Don't give in; they need to use their brain because it's the only way for them to learn how to survive in the world. Resist any temptation to jump in and supply the solution. Step away from the teenager. Be patient and wait. Engage your shields and if possible, move immediately to an adolescent free zone. Any effort to solve this problem must be their effort and they <u>must</u> find <u>their</u> solution. Anything you suggest will be met with disinterest, distain or perhaps outright hostility. From their perspective, <u>you</u> might be the problem. It's OK. Adolescents really do want to solve their own problems. Rest assured your teen will get all of the practice they can handle.

Teenagers are biologically driven to test their ideas out there in the world. Some of these ideas will work and others will not. Be careful as they enthusiastically describe their plan to fix the problem. You can feel your hair turning grey as you listen. You can feel the tension building in the back of your neck and your mouth becomes dry and you're thinking, *"I can't let this kid do that!"* In the past you may have jumped in at this point, but don't do that now. Did it feel good jump in and take over? Maybe. Did they appreciate it? I doubt it. There are two reasons for their lack of appreciation. In the first place your good intentions are viewed as intrusions and in the second place your teen interprets your input as a <u>criticism of their plan, therefore criticism of them.</u>

If you compulsively try to solve your children's problems, you are denying them opportunities to develop critical thinking and problem solving skills. They need to exercise their brain and they need to practice the analytical thinking that will insure their survival. Adolescence is a time when they need to develop creative problem-solving skills. They need to be developing their internal resources. The more opportunities they have to create their own solutions, the better they become at handling their lives when you are not around.

Now some of you might say, *"But they're going to make mistakes!"* Yes, they will make mistakes! Thank goodness! Mistakes are wonderful opportunities for them to learn? Isn't this is how we learned. You learn from your mistakes and if you don't, you repeat those mistakes them until you do learn. This can be a painful process but these lessons have been an important part of your growth and they will be an important part of your teen's growth.

If it alarms you that your teenager has little concern about a problem then it means <u>you</u> are probably overly concerned. It's their problem and <u>they</u> need to worry about it, not you. So stop worrying. At some point they will become worried enough to take action and deal with it. That is unless you hog all of the worry. Don't be a worry-hog; let them have their fair share.

Remind yourself that your son or daughter is ready for these experiences. The fears you have are <u>your</u> fears. *What? Me Worry?* frees you from worry that is not yours to have. Over the years I have learned that the more you worry about your kid's life, the less they worry about it? This is so common that I have developed a formula.

$$P + W = A - W$$

Where:

P = Parent,

W = Amount of Worry

and

A = Adolescent

In other words:

The *more* you worry, the *less* your kid worries.

Problem solving for teenagers is an *emotional* process and it's an *essential* process for them to master before they hit the streets. When your emotions become all clogged up in your kid's problems it causes their system to build up pressure, overheat, and eventually explode. If your teen suddenly explodes about a problem they are having then rejoice. In the case of our cartoon boy, this was not the first time he has had difficulty with Ms. Feeblemeister, but it <u>was</u> the first time he told his mother. His outburst is an indicator that he has been worried about this problem with this teacher for a while and he has finally come to a boiling point.

He has finally spilled the beans on what's been bugging him and now is a moment of choice for you. Some of those choices may include:

- Saying to him *"Stop whining and suck it up."*
- Ignoring him completely.
- Insisting he stop *"acting like a baby."*
- Tell him, in great detail, how you would deal with it.
- Say to him *"forget about it, she's not worth it."*
- Or you can let him worry about it and be supportive of his problem solving process.

Initially, your wonderful and amazing son or daughter will <u>not</u> be able to come up with a solution that meets your satisfaction. In fact, you might be appalled at some of the solutions they come up with. It's at those moments when you are at risk to jump in and take over. I know you can't help yourself. It's how parents are and besides, you have your reasons. Some of these reasons might be:

- *"That's the stupidest idea I have ever heard."*
- *"You can't just up and quit the class."*
- *"You wouldn't dare quit school!"*
- *"You had better not be serious about blowing up the teacher's car."*
- *"What if the police catch you?"*
- *"What do we tell neighbors if you do this?"*
- *"You know, I can I be sued."*
- *"If we get sued, there goes your college tuition."*

- And so on . . .

You're might be asking, *"So, what do I do now?"* This is a really good question and the most effective and powerful thing to do is this:

Know in your heart that your teenager is competent and capable of resolving any problem they encounter.

Yes, this is a radical idea, but if you imagine your kid is already capable and competent they really do become capable and competent. You may not believe it now, but your adolescent <u>really does</u> have the ability to solve their problems. All they lack is experience and because of this lack of experience, problems can be very stressful for them. This stress distorts their perception and makes them even more emotional. Don't worry about this. It's normal.

Your teen may believe this problem is the worst thing in the world and therefore, believe they are a complete failure. Is it any wonder why their solutions appear to be ill conceived? It's because they are ill conceived! How long did it take you to master life? I am in my 6th decade and there are still times when my life appears to be on the brink of disaster. This happens to everyone, including you. No matter how big or small the problem is, isn't it nice to know that life always regains its balance? Let them experience this on their own.

Now if you think your teenager is NOT having any problems, then look closer, you're not seeing the clues. Adolescents are driven to figure things out on their own, so they <u>need</u> problems. They need problems to learn how to trust themselves. They need to practice analyzing problems and then determine, on their own, viable solutions. They need to test their theories in order to develop confidence in their critical thinking skills. In this way they improve their problem solving abilities. This is the upside of falling down. Your teen needs to take risks. They are hard wired to boldly go where they have never gone before.

Right about now, I am hearing many of you screaming out in a frightful voice, *"But they'll get hurt!"* Yes! They may get hurt! But I know that you have lots of common sense and you would take appropriate action if their behavior is potentially dangerous. It is also true that teenagers know, at some level, what can happen when they make these decisions.

If you are a *worrier* then it's probably difficult for your son or daughter talk with you about their problems. It is not that they don't want your viewpoint and support; they don't want to worry you. When you use *What? Me Worry?* you build a bridge to better communication with your adolescent.

Don't be too quick to jump in and give them your solution. Let them explore ideas of their own. If your child discovers their approach doesn't work then they will be more open to your ideas. Who knows, perhaps they will come up with a viable solution and you can return to your supporting role. Let them run their heads into the metaphorical wall if they need to. You may have reminded your teen many times to *"Look before they leap."* Do they take your advice, probably not? As you know, teenagers have not yet mastered control over their impulses and ironically, this skill can only be learned by leaping into the abyss and discovering what happens. They are ready, whether you like it or not.

Each time your teen *hits a wall*, take time to listen to what they have to say about it. Explore with them the lessons inherent in such an experience. Think about how you can <u>follow</u> this conversation as opposed to <u>leading</u> the conversation down the road to <u>your</u> solution. By following the conversation you encourage your teen to tap into their internal resources.

When they finally clue you in on the problem, here are some things you can ask. Don't forget to breathe and remain cool, calm and collected.

- *How do you think this happened?*

- *How do you feel about what happened?*

- *How do you feel about your reaction?*

- *What could have you done differently?*

These mini-processing sessions will greatly reduce the amount of difficulty your teen experiences in the world. Running your head into the wall is a very effective way of learning what not to do. It certainly has worked for me. I am very familiar with the feeling of hitting the wall. I'm sure you are too.

When it comes to the health and safety of your children, we all agree that it is <u>your</u>

responsibility to make sure your kids survive until they reach adulthood *or* that magic age 18, whichever comes first. As you know, the majority of teenagers take risks and they participate in risky behavior whether you know it or not. I know that the physical safety of your children cannot be compromised and I agree. In the animal kingdom, most creatures fiercely protect their offspring. It's natural and appropriate to step in when there is clear and present danger. For example, your 14-year-old wants to sleep over at a friend's house with kids you don't know, and whose parents won't be at home. If your answer to a question like this is, *"No way, Jose"* then right on! This is a no brainer. If you suspect the activity(s) your teenager wants to do may harm them, then you need to set appropriate and firm limits with them. To your teen, a party is an opportunity to be on their own with their friends. It is very attractive and they are drawn to parties like a moth is drawn to a flame. This is probably what scares you.

Many acceptable activities such as playing sports have inherent risks of injury, however, given the social and physical benefits gained from participating in athletic programs this level of risk is acceptable to most parents. At times, however it is necessary to intervene in the myriad of dangers that all teenagers are vulnerable to, such as unsafe driving, assaults, bullies, unsafe sexual behavior, alcohol, drug abuse and so on. If your teen is engaging in dangerous behavior then do not pass go and do not collect $200. Get professional help immediately. Serious circumstances require serious actions. You must step in when it comes to the physical and emotional well-being of your children, whether they like it or not.

Fun Facts about Adolescents

Adolescents learn experientially. _This means that they learn best from life experience. They do not learn vicariously. They need real opportunities in the real world to test their ability to survive on their own. - Ray Erickson, 2001_

As your children grow, change and get older you need to change the way you parent them. You need to give them more responsibility for the management of their lives. This includes making their own decisions and accepting the consequences of those decisions.

With encouragement, they will apply any lessons learned to similar problems. If there is no clear and present danger then it is best to let them experiment with their ideas. Let them find out if their solution is viable or not. Allow them to test their decision so they can learn what works and what doesn't work.

When teenagers are given opportunities to test their theories and experience the consequences of their decisions, they are able to internalize the lesson. That is why classes which have an experiential factor are popular among teenagers. Adolescents do take in and learn from the advice of others, but for the most part, they need to get their hands dirty in order to grow from it.

Handy Insight

Think Jeopardy! When you're itching to comment on your teen's poorly thought out solution, remember to state that comment in the form a question.

What? Me Worry? doesn't mean you let your kid flop around out there without any support. It means that your role with your teen is now that of an advisor or consultant. The most effective way to do this is to ask questions as opposed to making statements. Here are some pointers to help you to follow the conversation with your teen:

- Base your first question on the last statement they made.
- Base your next question on their response to the first question and so on.
- Be curious about what they just shared.
- Use open ended questions and avoid "Yes or No" questions.
- Be open to anything they say.
- Seek understanding and clarification.

Questions like,

"What do you think Ms. Feeblemeister will do when you tell her that?"

encourages your teenager to look more closely at the consequences of their actions. By developing what I call an *other-awareness* teenagers are able to look beyond themselves and become sensitized to the feelings of others. Adolescents are notorious for their insensitivity towards other people. Because of the physical development of the adolescent brain, teenagers are less likely to take into account the feelings of others. Adolescents have very little *self-awareness* and even less *other-awareness.* This is because they tend to be *self-absorbed and obsessed with their life.*

All teens need assertiveness training. Learning this skill will help them tremendously for the rest of their life. Teenagers need to increase their self-awareness, improve their other-awareness and practice being assertive, every day. I discuss assertiveness training in greater detail in Chapter 7. Meanwhile, you can help your teen with questions like,

"How would you feel if someone said that to you?"

This is helpful in developing their ability to connect with their emotions and develop empathy for others. Teens may not always respond to such questions with thoughtful analysis and they may even shout back, *"I'd knock them out!"* Don't be alarmed, this is not how they feel. It's what they would like to do and not necessarily what they would do. Now, say to them,

127

"That's what you want to do, but how would you feel?"

As you ask, pay attention to how you feel but focus on how your teen feels. When you address your teen's feelings you help them connect their emotions to their actions. When your teen knows about the connection between their emotions and their behavior they begin to mature and grow up. They soon realize that when they feel crazy, they are crazy. With your love and support they will make the needed changes and ride off into the setting sun.

As difficult as it may be for you to tolerate your teen when they are in a highly agitated state, it is critical that you do. Keep yourself grounded in the knowledge that they have the ability to get through this. This sends a powerful message to your kids, even if you say nothing. Keep this in mind; your teenager is an amazing person! Let me repeat that.

Your teenager is an amazing person!

They are the future and if you lack faith in them, it is equivalent to lacking faith in the future. Your parents may have felt the same way about you and look how you turned out. Trust that all will be well and your teen eventually will surprise you with their resourcefulness and determination.

It is just as important to believe in your kids and their ability to learn and grow as it is to feed and clothe them. How many times have you heard your teen brag about their skill at video games or basketball or singing, yet not really believe it themselves? Actually, bragging is one of their provocative attempts to be validated.

Parents who worry too much are easily identified. They are the ones hovering over their kids. They are called *Helicopter Parents.* You can see their children shrinking in the background becoming fearful themselves as they try to avoid doing or saying anything that will worry their worrisome parent. You may even know some helicopter parents. Are you a *Helicopter Parent*?

Fun Facts about Adolescents

In their article, "How to Reduce Worry," Gavin de Becker, a family safety expert, makes this point: Parents enter into a contract with nature to keep that heart beating, to keep their children alive. That means parents recognize that children could die, yet whenever the thought comes into their heads, they quickly banish it. Writer Shawn Hubler says, "Preparedness is a funny thing; there's only so much of it a soul can stand. The problem with bracing for the worst is, you have to imagine it first." They go on to say: Children raised by chronic worriers may or not become victims of violence, but it is absolutely certain they will become victims of worry. In his brilliant book, The Heart of Man, Dr. Erich Fromm tells of a mother who is always interested in dark prognosis for her child's future, but unimpressed with anything favorable that occurs: "She does not harm the child in any obvious way, yet she may slowly strangle his joy of life."

This happens in families over and over. I get a call from a parent and in a matter of minutes I know that *worry* is the problem in the family, and not the teenager. That said, when these families come to therapy it is particularly important to re-establish healthy boundaries. Overly worrisome parents have little *self-awareness* and do not realize they are causing a problem. They believe strongly in their good intentions, regardless of the outcomes. They do not see their behavior as the catalyst for the problem. *Helicopter Parents* are focused outside of themselves and their world view is scary. These parents believe their teen's survival requires constant vigilance. Parents like this frequently over react to relatively minor problems and create a multitude of self-fulfilling prophecies.

Teenagers with parents who are overly worried about grades, will frequently end up doing poorly or failing in school, regardless of their academic abilities. Parents who hold onto irrational fears of drug or alcohol abuse often have teenagers who act out using alcohol or drugs regardless of their academic success. Teenagers with parents who worry obsessively about their safety may deliberately put themselves into dangerous situations or become victims of bullying or assault.

As previously mentioned; chronic worry creates self-fulfilling prophecies based upon the worry or fear. As a psychotherapist, I've noticed that parents with unreasonable worries or irrational fears increase the likelihood that the problem they are afraid of will manifest. In other words; *you get what you expect, so expect the best*. Take steps to reduce or eliminate any worry or fear as soon as possible. Keep your focus on what it would feel like if the best possible outcome has already occurred.

Your emotions are powerful communicators. Others can sense your mood, like you can sense the mood of others. In general, teenagers are highly intuitive when it comes to tuning into the feelings of their parents. Teenagers who live with an anxious or worried parent feel like they are doing everything they can to please that parent, yet the anxiety never goes away. These teenagers are put into a bind where they need to choose between their path or the path of pleasing their parents.

Teenagers in this situation may choose to give up on what they want for themselves to avoid causing their parents more worry. You can see their spirit cry as they slowly let go of their dreams. These kids are at higher risk for depression, self-destructive behavior and will often complain of somatic problems. On the other hand, many teens choose to act out in response to parental fears. These teens make conscious choices to engage in the behavior most feared by their parents. In other words, one teen <u>acts in</u>, restricting their exploration of the world, becoming fearful themselves and another teen <u>acts out</u>, diving into activities in defiance of their parents, becoming reckless and insensitive. In one case the teen becomes more like the worried parent and in the other case the teen becomes the worried parent's worst nightmare.

Neither direction has their best interest in mind and neither action results in growth and development. The best choice, the one nearest and dearest to your teenager's true self, lies somewhere in the middle.

Parents who worry excessively about their children are taking ownership and responsibility for their kid's lives. Because of this worry, *Helicopter Parents* micromanage their kids. Anxious and worried parents do have their reasons, which make sense to them, even if it makes no sense to others. Wanting your kids to do well is normal and healthy, but when you worry too much, it sends another message. That message is:

- I don't trust your judgment.

- I don't trust you to make the right decision.

- I don't trust you to know what is right for you.

- I don't trust your ability to do the right thing.

- I don't trust YOU.

Teenagers living under these conditions may become secretive and withhold information from the worried parent. They may even attempt to get the other parent to intervene for them. This is not an overt attempt to triangulate, although it may have the same effect. These cases are very complicated and families with an overly worried parent need professional help. There may even be a need for medication, not for the teen, but for the worried parent. High levels of anxiety suggest an anxiety or mood disorder.

As a family therapist, it is important to create a safe environment for these families. Often it becomes a matter of helping the adolescent accept that the worrisome parent may not change and then work with the teen to help them better understand what is going and how they can get their needs met. It's also important to assist the teen in establishing their boundaries and to teach them how to set limits with others. These teenagers have difficulty focusing on their needs because they are focused on the exaggerated needs of the worried parent. With support, the teenager learns how to reassure the worried parent. In this way they can focus on taking care of their business.

Developmentally, setting limits is a critical step for a teenagers' growth. Boundaries have been blurred by the worried parent and they are enmeshed with each other. In theory, if the teen performs up to standards then, the anxiety will lessen, but this rarely happens. Even if succeeds and there is less anxiety, the anxious parent will find something else to worry about. Teenagers in this situation feel tremendous pressure to be perfect. In this environment, mistakes are bound to occur creating even more worry. It is a real Catch-22.

Adolescents have a developmental need to separate and individuate from their families and this process is compromised when teenagers worry about their worried parent. When teenagers give up, they stop trying to please. They stop caring and may become hostile towards both parents. In doing so, they undermine their transition to adulthood. Teenagers who give up turn to other teenagers who have also given up. You know those kids. They are the ones you read about in the newspapers. They are the ones in the family down the street. But, they are not your kid, right? You be the judge. The point is; if you are a *Helicopter Parent* then you need to find ways to reduce your anxiety. Here are a few ideas:

- Develop a hobby for yourself

- Join a health and fitness club

- Read a book

- Get together with other parents of teenagers

- Meditate

- Take a yoga class

- Go dancing

- Go to the doctor because there may be a physical cause for your anxiety

- Go to therapy to learn non-medical ways to reduce your anxiety

Handy Insight

Your teen's behavior is not the cause of your anxiety any more than they are the cause of how tall you are. You are also not the cause of your teen's distress no matter what they say. Everyone, including you and I create our emotional state at any given moment. You've created this anxiety, only you can eliminate it.

Another form that worry takes is over-indulgence. One of the most common complaints I get about teenagers is how entitled and over-indulged they are. And there is plenty of evidence to back this up.

Look at all the *stuff* teenagers have these days. They've got computers, Nike's, iPods, I-Pads, iPhones, smart phones, designer clothing, motorcycles, Kindles, racing bikes, cars, flat screen TV's, DVD and MP3 players, etc, etc, etc. Yes Americans are spoiling their children. Even parents who cannot afford this madness get caught up in this *"gotta have it"* adolescent culture. As a consequence, our teenagers today appear to be shallow, self-absorbed, self-centered, demanding, disrespectful, and lazy. Did I say lazy? Let's not say lazy. Let's say misguided. Hmmmm....Now that I think about it, when haven't teenagers had these qualities?

If you are living in America, then you are living in an indulgent culture and your kids simply reflect that mindset. A great example of how adolescent life has changed since I was a teenager in the Sixties is to look at how proms have changed. When I was in high school, our junior and senior proms took place in the gymnasium.

Maybe your prom was in the gym as well. We would decorate the gym with crepe paper and streamers, everyone would pool their records, and a fellow student acted as the DJ. Proms in the new millennium have reached gigantic proportions. Instead of a gym, they are in a 5-Star hotel ballroom. If you live near the ocean proms may take place on a cruise ship. Sometimes, proms are at resorts 100 miles or more from their school, maybe even out of the country. Imagine that! Even if the prom is still in the gym, there is the mandatory limousine to and from the prom. There are the after prom parties at hotels where kids rent an entire floor at the hotel. Each year the prom has to be bigger and grander than last years. It's absolutely insane! What is wrong with this picture? *What? Me Worry?* is an excellent tool to combat this trend. The prom is not your concern; it's your kid's concern. Don't buy into this ever escalating pattern that is costing your family an arm and a leg.

Get involved with the parents of your teenager's friends and take active steps to work with the school officials to begin to bring this annual event under control. You will need to involve the students of course; it is their prom after all. But the trend of having to indulge your kids with all the latest gadgets, fashions, lavish proms, senior trips and so on creates an illusion that one can only be happy if they consume at a pace that puts everyone into debt. How many of you have borrowed money to pay for that prom dress, or the senior trip to Mexico?

What I'm saying here is this; over-indulgent parents are oftentimes worried parents and they have very little tolerance for emotional discomfort. They don't want to see their child disappointed and they don't want their child to *"lack"* for anything. The rationale for indulgence is evidenced by the following examples.

Parent Rationalizations

- I don't want my kid to suffer like I did.
- They're good kids; this is how I show them my love and appreciation.
- I just can't say no to them.
- Just this once, but you had better get your grades up.
- I can afford it, so why not?

Adolescent Rationalizations

- Everyone is going to be there
- I'll die of embarrassment if I have to wear that.
- Everyone has one.
- Everyone is doing it.
- Everyone will make fun of me.

What? Me Worry? supports your teen by letting them have these problems. They will survive wearing Acme instead of Nike.

Indulging your children is not about the needs of your children. It is about your needs. Granted, teens are not complaining about their new iPod or their new designer jeans or their new BMW. But do they really need all of this opulence? I seriously doubt it. *What? Me Worry?* helps you to stay grounded as you and your teen figure out how to split the difference between what they want and what you are willing to give.

There is a wonderful side effect of this negotiating process. When your teen realizes that you are not going to give them your credit card, they might decide to get a job or to do extra work around the house in order to earn the money to indulge themselves. This is much healthier than being indulged by you. It's a win-win situation. You get to save some of your hard earned cash and they get to learn the benefits of working for something they want.

I noticed a pattern over the years and it is described below with this formula.

$$P - W = A + I$$

Where: P = Parent

W = Worry

A = Adolescent

and

I = Industrialness

In other words

The less worried the parents are, the more industrious their teenager is.

Hmmmm… The less you worry about your kid, the more ambitious and industrous they become. Imagine that! If this is true and I've seen this happen in many families, then your teenager really can handle a part-time job or extra chores around the house <u>and</u> keep up with their classes. Instead of you worrying about your teenager's life, *What? Me Worry?* lets your teen worry about their life. This is good for their growing and expanding brains. You may even learn that your previously clueless teenager can be quite creative, resourceful, and motivated to do what it takes to get what they want.

A friend and colleague of mine along with his wife raised two wonderful young men who have gone to college and are now living on their own. They may appear to be just as indulged and self-absorbed as any other young adult but they truly know how to work for what they want. The most influential factor was this; the purchase of all big ticket items, like bicycles, motorcycles, cars, proms or senior trips and so on was based on an agreement the family had established early on. My friend chipped in for half the cost, but the boys needed to come up with the other half of the money. These kids took on extra work around the house or found jobs to earn the money to buy that bicycle, motorcycle or car.

My friend recognized their inherent drive to go after what they want, and turned it into an opportunity for them to learn how to work. Look to your own experience to validate this approach and I think you will agree. The important thing to keep in mind is that the more opportunities teens have to engage the world, the better they do at life. This means that you won't need *What? Me Worry?* because you will know, deep down in your heart, that your teen is capable and competent.

Chapter 7
Testing 1-2-3 Testing

*"The young always have the same problem-
how to rebel and conform at the same time.
They have now solved this by defying their
parents and copying one another." ~ George
Chapman*

        "Look at me when I'm talking to you!"
If you have ever said this to your teen then
you're a typical parent. The problem with such a
statement is it turns off your teen's ability to
hear anything you say after that. *Testing 1-2-3
Testing* is a direct approach that you can apply
when communicating important information to
your teen. Imagine you are telling your teen a
few important details and suddenly their eyes
role up into their heads. Ignore this crass
attempt to distract you and ask,

> *"What do you understand about what I just
> said?"*

If their answer makes no sense and it's obvious
they weren't listening, take a deep breath and
calmly repeat or rephrase what you just said and
follow up with,

> *"Now, what do you understand about what I
> just said?"*

This technique is useful during *The Meeting* after a *Hit and Run*. Use *Testing 1-2-3 Testing* whenever you get the *eye roll* or your teen has entered a trance.

Do not take anything your teen says or does, personally. It's not about you.

It's normal for teenagers to see you and other adults as lower life forms. They pay little attention to what parents, teachers, and other grownups say directly to them. Teenagers are simply not interested in what you are talking about, unless you are talking about them. How often have you said to your teen, *"Did you hear what I said?"* and they look at you, nod their head and say, *"Of course I heard you"*. Then, as you walk away feeling good about yourself and how well you and your kid are communicating, you suddenly realize they didn't hear a word you said. Where were they when I explained, in painstaking detail, my plan for their success? Hmph, kids."

Where were they? They were right in front of you, passively unengaged in a conversation that was going only one direction: from you to them. Because of your enthusiasm, you may have missed the subtle signs of disinterest, like how they were watching TV, talking on the telephone, playing a video game or eating a snack. As mentioned earlier, teenagers will invest every ounce of energy they have pursuing something they want, but when it comes to something you want, well that's a different story. In general, teenagers <u>are not</u> interested in what you have to say. They <u>are</u> interested in being left to themselves or being allowed to hang out with their friends.

It is up to you to ensure that communication has actually occurred and *Testing 1-2-3 Testing* is a very effective way of making sure that what you say gets heard, and understood. For instance, when you ask the question, *"Did you clean your room?"* The inevitable answer is, *"Of course I cleaned my room!"* In <u>their</u> eyes it is clean, but in your eyes, it's a lot closer to the proverbial "pig sty."

Handy Insight
Teenagers need adults to draw a map for them.

Communication problems are resolved easily by being very clear about what you expect. Make a list, write them down and be sure to include all the details, <u>even those you consider to be common sense.</u> When working with teenagers, if it is not on the list, then it doesn't get done and if you don't follow-up, then you may find many tasks on the list not completed.

Adolescents have very little world experience and therefore do not see or hear things the way you do. You know the expression, *"One man's junk is another man's treasure."* In this case, the parent's *"pig sty"* is a teenager's *"safe haven."* This chapter is not about getting your teenager to clean their room; it's about communicating clearly with them. *Testing 1-2-3 Testing* guarantees you are heard and heard correctly. When you ask your teen what they've heard you say, you help them become better listeners.

Here's another great thing about this tip. It's actually two tips in one. The flip side of *Testing 1-2-3 Testing* is called *1-2-3 Testing 1-2-3.* In this case, it is you who tells your teen what you heard instead of your teen telling you what they heard.

Imagine that you've been patiently listening to your teen and have done well not to interrupt while at the same time attempting to decipher the point they are making. When you think you understand, raise your finger (no, not that finger) and wait. If and when they take a breath or pause, use this opportunity to give them a recap and summarize what you've heard. In a discussion it may sound something like this:

"Now, let me see if I understand. What I hear you saying is this; the reason you're home late from school is because zombies attacked, right?" And you needed to stay and help the principal and teachers protect the other students from being killed by the zombies. Is there anything I've missed here?"

By sharing your understanding up to that point, you are demonstrating that what they are saying is important, <u>plus</u> you model the behavior you expect from them. For example, your son's response to your summary may be, *"Nooooo, they weren't Zombies, they were living dead people"* (like you don't know the difference)! This type of misunderstanding happens every day between adolescents and their parents.

Handy Insight
Many miscommunications that occur between teenagers and parents can be cleared up easily by giving each other

feedback about what you hear the other person say.

However, if these miscommunications are not handled well, they can turn into *Nuclear Chain Reactions* and things get worse, much worse.

Naturally, your teen is going to think this is stupid and may take the opportunity to let you know just how stupid it is. Teens love to parrot back your exact words as proof that they heard you. Often there will be just a hint of irritation in their voice. This does not mean they understand what you are saying and even though they are mocking you, <u>don't take this personally</u>. Teenagers are not very experienced at communicating clearly, and their tone of voice simply reflects their desire to be left alone. It has nothing to do with you so pay no attention to this *attitude.* Go ahead and asked them again,

"No, really, in your own words what do you understand about what I've been talking about?

As a psychotherapist who has worked with teenagers for over 3 0 years, I have found *1-2-3 Testing 1-2-3* to be a valuable tool that helps me to truly understanding what adolescents are saying. Most teens appreciate that I am so interested in their lives. This makes them feel good about themselves and supports their efforts to understand their world and their relationship with it. *1-2-3 Testing 1-2-3* is a great addition to your communication toolbox. Use it often.

146

Fun Facts about Adolescents

The adolescent is easily distracted from tasks he or she does not desire to perform. Normally, attention span varies greatly depending upon the child's or adolescent's interest and skill in the activity, so much so that a short attention span for a particular task may reflect the child's skill or interest in that task. The American Academy of Pediatrics. "The Classification of Child and Adolescent Mental Diagnoses in Primary Care." Diagnostic and Statistical Manual for Primary Care (DSM-PC), Child and Adolescent Version. Elk Grove Village, IL: American Academy of Pediatrics; 1996

I don't get it, but for some strange reason teenagers assume that you are angry with them after asking them to do something for the 12th time. This is not a real problem, this is only a test. If you blow your cool, you fail.

All teenagers test the limits and expectations of their parents, and they will do this in a variety of curious ways. One popular way to test limits is to put the task off. Procrastination is one of the easiest ways to push back on parental limits. It takes no energy at all to put something off.

Testing 1-2-3 Testing helps you hold your teen accountable for the commitments they make. They know precisely what you expect from them, you've told them a hundred times. It's their job to take care of these commitments, not yours. Of course, procrastination is not limited to *Teen World*; it's a cornerstone of family life in *Grownup World* as well. Teenagers don't procrastinate on purpose, just to disobey you. They are not defying you when they put something off. In fact, it has nothing to do with you; they just don't want to do that job in the first place. In your teen's eyes, you don't understand how busy *Teen World* is. Their time is taken up with activities like school, homework, chores, family activities, sleeping, eating, hanging out with their friends, eating again and so on. Why can't you see they don't have time to do what <u>you</u> need them to do?

Adolescents are baffled when grownups don't understand how busy they are. Your teen may automatically say *"I'll do it later"* then conveniently forget to do it altogether. This is their way of telling you they are too busy to take care of it now or at any other time. *Are you blind? Can't you see I'm busy?* The real reason for procrastinating is simple: they don't want to do whatever it is you want them to do.

Most procrastinating people put the least desirable task at the bottom of the list but experts suggest you do the opposite and tackle the ugliest job first. Then the other chores will be much easier to do. As much as you are keenly aware of how your teen puts things off, they in turn, are equally aware of any procrastination on your part, especially if it directly affects them, like taking them to the mall. Be aware of any procrastination on your part and take corrective action. It is important that you are not a *"do as I say, not as I do"* parent.

If the task is important enough and the job needs to be completed right away, then a little NFTD or *No Fun Till Done* can help light a fire under their chair. Even though both of you are human and in spite of all the drama, the important things do get done. Don't let procrastination rob you and your teen of the joy of accomplishment.

Your teen's procrastination is not as simple as avoiding something. Putting off an important task can be an indicator that your teen does not understand what to do or how to begin. Naturally adolescents want you to think of them as capable and competent, but they are afraid of making mistakes and disappointing you. Everything has to be perfect or it is not done at all. I know, this doesn't explain their room, but nevertheless, this fear causes them to believe that you will judge them harshly. Therefore, if they don't start it, they won't mess it up. (Yes, many teenagers really do think like this.) By avoiding the task, they avoid proving to you their incompetence. Besides, if they put it off long enough, maybe you'll forget about it or it will magically go away. This is why believing in your teen is important.

Chronic procrastination is a sign that something is lurking below the surface, like low self-esteem, an anxiety disorder or depression. It could also be nothing more than manipulation by your teen to get out of doing the chore. Whatever it means, do not make the mistake of labeling procrastination as *laziness*. I've never met a lazy teenager. I know what you're thinking, *"You haven't met my kid."*

Blame it on their brain. Each day your teen has between 60,000 and 80,000 thoughts in their head and most of these thoughts are attached to problems they are having or problems they want to avoid. Nevertheless, your teen's brain is a very busy place. This is a big reason why adolescents communicate so poorly. In addition, most of the communication coming from teenagers is emotionally triggered. As you know, emotions are powerful, especially fear, anxiety, or confusion. If your teen chronically puts things off, then seek a deeper understanding. Get some help if you need to.

Handy Insight

When you use Testing 1-2-3 Testing you help your son or daughter learns how to stop their random and chaotic thoughts and focus on one thing. You help them to be in the moment with you. What a wonderful gift!

Your teen is always thinking and much of their brain is concentrating on things that you believe are a waste of time and energy. Don't despair. Let them think all they want. It's OK. They are practicing new cognitive skills; new critical thinking abilities and they are fine-tuning their expanding brain power. I know it may look like your teen is not thinking, but they are. Really, they are. So what in the world could they be thinking about? Adolescence is a time when teenagers review, renew, revise and reject the entire spectrum of issues and events affecting their lives.

Here is a partial list of what teenagers think about.

- Parents
- Parenting
- Family life
- Friends
- Boyfriends/Girlfriends
- Having sex
- Not having sex
- Becoming a parent
- Not becoming a parent
- Peers (other kids)
- School
- Teachers
- Homework
- Money
- What's going on Friday night?
- Smoking
- Alcohol
- Drugs
- College
- Career
- Politics
- Community events
- Regional events
- National events

- World events
- Race relations
- Love
- Peace
- War
- Justice
- Their future
- God or no God

When you look carefully at this list, it's no wonder your kid is overwhelmed at times. Like your teen, you too, have a lot going on in your head, but you have much more experience with this chatter. According to the Family Affirmation Network the average person has 60,000 thoughts per day and *80% of these thoughts are negative.* Ouch! It's no wonder teenagers have such a difficult time listening! Their heads must be ready to explode.

Along with their newfound ability to contemplate life, comes the tendency for teenagers to constantly evaluate their relationship to others and the environment. Given the egocentric and self-absorbed nature of adolescence, they form many negative and self-limiting beliefs about themselves and life, such as the belief that they don't have power and control over their lives. This belief partially explains why teenagers are so stressed out. *When your teen believes they are powerless they have thoughts of powerlessness. These limiting thoughts create feelings of powerlessness which attract situations proving to them and everyone else, just how powerless they are.* Talk about a slippery slope! The advantage you have over your teen is your experience. Life has a way of knocking off the sharp edges and over time, if you pay attention, your life becomes a lot smoother.

As you know, it takes a conscious effort to focus on one thing for any length of time. But you may not realize just how difficult it is for your teenager to shift the gears and focus on what you are saying. Shifting mental gears for teenagers is like getting off a merry-go-round while it's still moving. They may stumble a bit as they hit the ground but they soon recover and are back on their feet. Being patient with your teen is good for you and shifting their focus is good for them.

One reason your teen may appear not to be listening, is because of all the noise in their heads. It may not be readily apparent, but there is a possibility they can't hear you <u>because</u> of the racket going on between their ears. <u>Or</u>, they simply were not listening. The truth is it doesn't matter why they aren't listening. You need to get their attention first and give them a moment to shift gears. It's very important to get their attention before you say anything and if you can get eye contact before speaking, that's the best.

Handy Insight

Always get your teen's attention
<u>before</u> you speak.

Now that you have their attention, be sure to watch for signs that they have lost their concentration. Strike while the iron is hot! Make it short, simple and sweet, like the *Hit and Run*.

Imagine you've been talking with your teen for 5 minutes when you notice them becoming distracted. Pay attention to this subtle sign. When they look at their watch or their eyes glaze over or they roll over and go back to sleep you've reached the end of their attention span. This is the time to use *Testing 1-2-3 Testing.* When these signs appear, you have your teen right where you want them. You have their attention, well, sort of. Stay focused and say it! Say it now before it's too late! Use *Testing 1-2-3 Testing*, before your teen has completely checked out! Ready? Do it now! Calmly say,

"What do you hear me saying to you?"

Good. Now smile at them and wait for their response. Be sure to remain calm and don't get agitated when your teen lacks interest in your sage advice. This behavior is NOT about you, so don't take it personally.

Fun Facts about Adolescents

Dr. Robert Sylwester, author of The Adolescent Brain: Reaching for Autonomy *(Corwin Press, 2007) and an Emeritus Professor of Education at the University of Oregon talks about the relationship between attention and adolescent interests in a January, 2008 interview by Alvero Fernandez of www.sharpbrains.com Dr. Sylwester states, "The important thing for adults to do is to carefully observe an adolescent's interests and abilities, and insert challenges that move maturation forward at a reasonable level. If you push too fast, you end up with a stressed out adolescent. If you do not challenge sufficiently, you end up with a bored adolescent. No magic formula exists for getting this just right. In short, parents and educators need to pay attention to observe where adolescent's interests and abilities lie, and engage them with experiences that will enable them to move forward."*

The Fun Fact above refers to normal adolescents. If it looks like your teen's is not listening to you, then they probably aren't. This is not a reflection on you. Their lack of interest is their thing and it changes on a day-to-day, moment-to-moment basis. Teenagers do focus and pay attention to things that interest them, but do not focus on things that do not interest them.

Sometimes teenagers will react strongly to *Testing 1-2-3 Testing* and may even storm out of the room in a huff. Remember when your teen blows up or loses control, it has nothing to do with you. This kind of reaction is all about them and their busy, growing brain. Do not take any of this behavior personally. Do not become irritated with your teen. Practice patience because a complete breakdown in communication occurs if both of you get irritated, and you don't want that to happen. These conditions are the breeding ground of *Nuclear Chain Reactions.*

How long does it take your teen to *turn off* to your wonderfully wise, poignant, profound and appropriate advice that you so freely offer? At no cost to them! One minute, two minutes, ten minutes, ten seconds? Remember, their behavior is not about you. This is what young, growing brains do; their minds wander when under-whelmed and crash when they are overwhelmed.

If you haven't noticed that your teen has lost interest, you waste your time and energy repeating yourself over and over . . . . and over. Now is the time for you to ask that wonderful blob of protoplasm, your adolescent, this question,

"What do you understand about what I just said?"

Asking for understanding gives them a chance to develop mental and verbal organizational skills. When you ask the very popular, but incredibly ineffective question,

"Did you hear what I said?"

Your teen will look at you and say *"Yeah."* This requires virtually no mental organizing skill, but it's the fastest way for them to get back to doing what they were doing, before you so rudely interrupted them.

When you ask, *"What do you understand about what I just said?"* it requires your teen to review the information you provided and organize it into a plausible response. The amount of intellectual energy your teen spends on this activity alone is the equivalent of a mental pentathlon. Yes, it's like an Olympic event! It's good exercise for their brain. No wonder they need to take a nap after these discussions. They have brain fatigue.

So, what are the signs that your teen's audio receiver is encountering interference? Here are a few off the top of my head. How many have you noticed in your household?

Verbal cues:

- Do we have to talk about this now?
- What is it NOW!?
- Whatever.....
- Duh?!
- I've gotta go...
- Mommmm!!!
- Daaaaaddd!!!
- I can't right now! Can't you see I'm busy?

Non-verbal cues:

- The Eye Roll (a classic)
- Yawning (obvious, but a teen favorite)
- Looking up and away from you
- Looking down and away from you
- Closing their eyes and drumming their fingers
- Eyes glazing over (gone into trance)
- Looking at their watch or a clock
- Picking up a magazine
- Checking their voicemail
- Texting or emailing friends about what they have to put up with

As you may have noticed, teenagers are very creative in their efforts to get back to their lives, free of parental discussion and interruptions. <u>Never take your teen's statements or gestures personally, even if your teen intends them to be personal.</u> Be thankful you're not in their shoes, much less in their heads. Be grateful that you can use *Testing 1-2-3 Testing* to help their big, growing brains to become better at responding to the world at large.

Handy Insight

Parents have incredible power over the lives of their children. Teenagers see parents as bosses of their lives.

By consistently using *Testing 1-2-3 Testing* you say to your teen that you want them to understand you and you want to understand them. <u>Understanding is the result of good communication.</u> Over time you might even see the coup d'état of communication. This is when your teen uses *Testing 1-2-3 Testing* with a friend, a sibling or even you. This is clear evidence that they have been listening and understanding. So, if your teenager is using *Testing 1-2-3 Testing* to make sure you understand what they are saying, then kudos to you.

Your teen may not show it or say it, but you are very important to them. Even though they tell you to *"Get your big nose out of my business."* they get nervous when you don't show any interest in what they are doing. Go figure. You know how this feels. I bet there have been times at work when you're telling your boss about a new account and he is too busy and distracted to pay much attention, much less appreciate the effort you made. Then, when you finish your report, your boss says, *"Did you call the Johnson account?"* You may have felt dismissed, perhaps even hurt and angry. You know they heard you, but do they understand how important this account is to you? It doesn't feel good to be dismissed by those you hold in high esteem or those whom you believe have power and control over your life.

This is how your teen feels when you don't show an active interest in their lives. This doesn't mean you need to listen to their music or wear their fashions, but it does mean that it's important take an interest in their world. New sneakers, $120; new CD, $15; your teenager sharing with you what happened today, priceless. <u>Be grateful when they are telling you something, anything, about their lives.</u>

Assertiveness Gets You What You Want

While it may not be difficult for you, it is very difficult for many people to assert themselves, particularly with authority figures. It is infinitely more difficult for teenagers to be assertive. As you know, being a teenager is stressful and at times, this stress causes them to fly off the handle. When they do, it's an opportunity to help them practice being *assertive*. You know how important it is to be assertive in this world. Teaching your teen this valuable skill will benefit them for the rest of their lives. And if they can be assertive with you when they really need to be, they can be assertive with any authority figure they encounter.

Handy Insight
Assertiveness meets your needs <u>and</u> respects the rights and feelings of others.

When your teen does fly off the handle, it may feel good to them, but it feels really bad to you. Teach your teen that getting angry doesn't work with bosses and spouses, but if they are assertive, they create a win-win situation. This means everyone gets what they want. This is the whole point of being assertive. I know this makes sense to you, but it is way too time consuming for your teen. After all, what's wrong with using high pitched whiny demands until you give in? This has worked for them so far?

The easiest way to teach teenagers how to be assertive is to show them how to use *I Messages*. An *I Message* does not use the word *"you."* There is no *"you"* in an *I Message*. Look at the examples below.

- Instead of saying *"You're grounded for life!"* you can say ***"I'm so upset right now; I cannot even be in the same room."***

- Instead of saying *"Don't you talk to me like that!"* you can say **"I don't like how I'm being spoken to."**

Normally assertiveness is used when communication is problematic, but it is especially effective when used to reinforce your teen's positive behavior. In these cases assertiveness has the *you* and sounds like this.

- *"I really appreciate the job you did on your room today."*

- *"I'm so proud of the effort you made to help your brother."*

- *"It is so good to be able to talk with you like this."*

The *you* is emphasized because you want your teen to be clear that you are talking about them and you feel good about it.

When you prepare for a *Hit and Run* you are being assertive with a very specific message. When you use *Testing 1-2-3 Testing* with your teenager, you are also being assertive. Assertiveness satisfies your need to get clarity and understanding while at the same time respecting your teen's right to be treated humanely.

Your teen may think you are being ridiculous and wasting their valuable time; time that could be spent doing anything else besides reciting back to you what was said. When you ask your teen, *"Did you hear what I said?"* much to your amazement, they recite back to you, word for word, everything you said. Impressive, but did you get the feeling they understood? Not really. This is why it is important to <u>ask what they understand</u> about what you said.

When your teen presses their replay button acknowledge their ability to hear you, remind them that you expect more than that. You expect them to understand and be clear on what is being conveyed. You can say something like,

"Well, I guess you did hear me, but what do you understand about what I said?"

Testing 1-2-3 Testing and *1-2-3 Testing 1-2-3* are two very simple methods to keep the channels of communication open between you and your teen. These tools also come in handy when communicating with your spouse, your coworkers, your friends or anyone else that you need to be crystal clear with. It feels good to be heard and understood. *Testing 1-2-3 Testing* creates more trust and better communication. When you can hear <u>and</u> understand your teen it builds their self-esteem and improves your relationship with them. So use this tip whenever you are sending or receiving important information. What do you have to lose?

On your mark, get set, go..... Assert yourself with *Testing 1-2-3 Testing.*

The Judo Approach

Chapter 8
The Judo Approach

At fourteen you don't need sickness or death for tragedy. ~Jessamyn West

Eventually, you <u>will</u> be blamed for ruining your teen's life. They may rage and curse and jump up and down, but if you are prepared for this inevitable assault, the hurt and anger can be disarmed very effectively. *The Judo Approach* recommends that you go with your teen's feelings instead of counter-attacking or defending yourself. Statements such as, *"Wow, you're really angry with me, what's going on?"* validate your teen's feelings and encourage discussion.

Telling your teen to calm down and demanding respect at these times cuts off communication. Instead, remain calm and listen carefully with the intent to understand. (See Chapter 10) Let your teen know that their opinions matter to you. *The Judo Approach* opens the door to problem solving. After the problem is solved, you can go back and address your concerns about any disrespectful behavior.

The Judo Approach is a powerful way to resolve conflict. By going with the flow of your teen's energy, you will effectively disarm them. They've built up a huge head of steam and they are embroiled in their emotions. They are ready for a fight. <u>Don't get sucked in!</u> Why would you want to stick your nose into the mess they've made? Remember that Halloween night many years ago and the doorbell rang. When you opened the door, there's a paper bag on fire. Do you really want to *stomp* on it again? Then back off. Step away from the teenager.

The Judo Approach surprises your teen because they are braced for a fight and armed for battle. They've had enough of you and they don't expect you to admit any wrongdoing. When you take responsibility for yourself, it surprises them. This is the last thing they expect.

The Judo Approach helps you to dodge power struggles when your teen expects you to argue with them. Yes they may have a problem with you, but it's <u>their</u> problem, not <u>yours</u>. Now <u>you</u> may have a problem with their behavior, their language or their tone of voice, but these things are not the problem. These behaviors are indicators of the problem and how strongly your teen feels about it, they are not the problem. When your son or daughter is angry with you *The Judo Approach* gently allows both of you to get to a place where you can express yourselves honestly. When the real problem is resolved you can go back and address the problem of their conduct. This is an opportunity to teach them how to be more assertive.

In the meantime, when your teen is feeling overwhelmed there is nothing you can do or say to calm them down, so go with the flow. This means validating their feelings and experiences. Adolescents are often <u>unaware</u> of their emotions, much less be able to express them appropriately. When you confirm your teen's right to be angry, their anger subsides or disappears altogether. Help your teen to identify the feelings beneath the anger. This helps your teen to respond to stressful events without becoming overwhelmed and resorting to anger.

Adolescents expect adults to minimize, even ridicule their viewpoints. Teenagers firmly believe that grownups are unable to admit doing anything wrong. But....when you admit you're wrong, magic happens. Teenagers also believe adults think they know it all and don't take them seriously. (They could be right here.) All of their lives, teenagers have lived in the shadow of the adults around them. They need an adult's permission to do almost anything and by the time they become adolescents; these young people are fed up with parental control.

Parents and teachers, bless their hearts; have a reputation of being notorious "know it all's." By this I mean, for whatever reasons, teachers and parents have difficulty admitting to mistakes. Perhaps they believe admitting to mistakes makes them appear fallible, foolish or not worthy of respect. Actually, just the opposite is true. When you make a mistake and don't take responsibility, it erodes the trust and respect you have built up with your kid. Teenagers know when you're not being honest with them. As mentioned in Chapter 1, your kids are much too wise to fall for such obvious attempts to cover up a mistake.

Children are told to take responsibility for their behavior nearly every day by well-meaning parents, teachers, and other adults in their lives. Frequently, however, these same adults don't take personal responsibility for themselves. I call this the *"do as I say, not as I do"* syndrome. When these kids are fortunate enough to encounter adults who actually walk their talk, they are relieved to know that not <u>all</u> adults are the same.

Think about some of the misleading statements you have told your children. I'm not talking about your answers to questions like, *"Does Santa Clause really exist?"* I'm talking about being honest with your kids about life when they most need the truth.

By the time your teen DOES confront your hypocrisy; they have put a lot of thought into the problem and have been experiencing it for a long time. Their confrontation gives you a golden opportunity to solidify your relationship. Yes, it may look pretty rocky right now but any defensive posturing on your part will only escalate the problem. If your teen is hopping mad at you, it is the perfect time to use *The Judo Approach.*

Imagine this scenario: You arrive home from work after a long day. You are tired and looking forward to a peaceful evening at home. As soon as you walk through the door, your daughter confronts you. She is consumed with frustration and anger, and it's all directed at you! What do you do, now? What have you done in the past? Many parents react to their yelling teens with anger and yell back at them, creating even more anger and hostility. In families like this, he who yells loudest wins. Don't be this family. When your teen's anger and frustration are met with your anger and frustration they become intimidated and feel powerless. Then before you know it, this dangerous mix of emotions turns into a *Nuclear Chain Reaction.*

Handy Insight

Remember! In your teen's eyes, YOU have ALL the power and THEY have NONE.

You may be tired, frustrated, and confused, but if you are caught off guard it's extremely important not to get defensive. Defensiveness leads to even more anger. It is also a good idea to buy some time, clear your head and get a better idea about what's going on. After all, you've just been accosted by a lunatic disguised as your daughter! This is where all of your practice with *Shields Up, Scotty* really pays off.

Remain quiet and calm. Breathe slowly and deeply until you are free of any defenses. When you're ready to speak, simply say, *"You're right."* And wait for a moment. If you need more information, ask for it, but ask out of curiosity, like that time at work when your coworker went off on you. You have tremendous power over the life of your teen and they expect you to be unwilling to see their point of view. Because of this belief, teens avoid dealing with problems of any kind until they feel so much pressure that a tiny little thing causes a huge emotional meltdown. Be assured that when this happens, it WILL be your fault, but <u>do not take this personally.</u> This is a common adolescent perception. They think, *"It can't possibly be my fault, so it must be my parent's fault."* You may have noticed this tendency.

Since your daughter feels powerless with adults she may blame adults for her problems. In this case you. If you're lucky she is blaming that other parent, you know, the bad parent. I'm sure you've heard your daughter say in an exasperated tone, *"I can't believe what Dad did!"* Does it matter what Dad did? Not really, that's between your daughter and her father. Remember, it's their problem. Your job is not to rescue her. Why is she telling you now? You are hearing it now because you're the <u>safe</u> parent at <u>this</u> moment. Tomorrow you may be in Dad's shoes, but that's tomorrow. Right now, what does your daughter needs from you?

In your most calm, patient and wise parent voice, you ask, *"What happened?"* The reply may be something like, *"He embarrassed me in front of all my friends."* You might be tempted to ask what seems to be the next logical question, *"What did he do now?"* However, this seemingly innocent question does nothing to solve the problem and may cause even more distress for your daughter. As interested as you might be in the details of what happened, it's really none of your business. If you get into this line of questioning you run the risk of being drawn into a <u>Triangulation</u>, a dynamic that pits one parent against the other. It is very dangerous and I will talk more about it later in this chapter. When using *The Judo Approach* in this situation, you might say, *"What was that like for you?"*

The solution to your daughter's problem is not in the details of what happened and by wisely avoiding the details, you can now focus on her feelings. They are not hard to get to; her emotions are bubbling up to the surface and looking for an opening to come out. When you ask, *"What was that like for you?"* you get to the heart of the matter immediately. In this case, your daughter may say, *"It was the worst thing that has ever happened in my life!"* Stay with it, you are doing fine. Now ask again, *"What was THAT like for you?* She responds*, "I thought I would die!"* Each time you ask what it was like for her, you get closer and closer to the real problem. Eventually, you may hear, *"I don't think Dad loves me."* Bingo!

This is good, but what do you do now? This is where *The Judo Approach* comes in again. It's time to empathize with your kid and say something like:

"I'm so sorry; it must be awful to think your father doesn't love you. It would really bother me if I felt that way."

At this point, you might notice a shift or change in their affect. If they are open to a hug, give them a hug. If they are not, then don't and maintain your distance. Quietly being there is comforting. She will be relieved to know that you understand and are not taking anybody's side.

Be sure to use open-ended questions as opposed to *yes* or *no* questions. Do not use *leading* questions that attempt to lure her into doing what you think she needs to do. *The Judo Approach* allows you to gently help her find her own solutions to the problem. If she happens to come up with the same solution as you, that's great. Either way, acknowledge her efforts and validate her concerns about talking with her father. At the same time encourage her to talk with Dad as soon as possible. Your daughter will feel empowered to know that you support her and have not taken sides. Let her know you're an expert at talking with Dad about sensitive subjects and perhaps you can help.

It may also be helpful to prepare Dad for the upcoming discussion with his daughter. This can get tricky and has great potential for triangulation. You must be very clear that the problem is NOT his problem to solve. You must also be clear with Dad that he needs to wait until his daughter approaches him. If he goes to her first and says,

"Your mother told me that you don't think I love you."

Boom! Now you have instant triangulation and your daughter will feel betrayed by you. There are several very good reasons for her to have control over when to approach Dad:

- She may not be ready to talk with Dad when he wants to talk.

- She will feel betrayed if you go behind her back

- Triangulation can easily occur

- The problem with Dad can get worse

- A new, bigger problem is created

When you do talk with Dad, tell him about *The Judo Approach* so he can prepare to be empathetic, have an open heart and truly listen to his daughter.

Let's take a closer look at triangulation. There are 3 requirements for triangulation to occur in families. First, there needs to be a <u>Victim</u> and naturally if there is a victim there needs to be a <u>Victimizer</u> or <u>Persecutor</u>. The third leg of the triangle is the <u>Rescuer</u>.

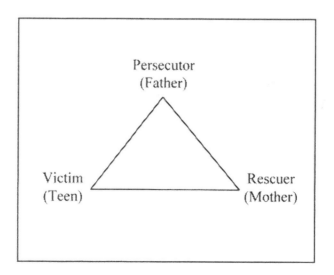

The illustration above shows how these roles are created in a family to form triangulation. In the scenario above your teen has taken the <u>Victim</u> role. This is a common role for adolescents because they believe they are powerless with adults, especially parents. Her complaint about Dad puts Dad in the <u>Persecutor</u> role whether he knows it or not. He may also be innocent to a large degree.

You may have a strong and compelling urge to do something to help your teen. You may even want to go to her father and demand that he make amends immediately. If so, you are the <u>Rescuer</u>. Your daughter may expect you to take on the problem and go talk with Dad for her. Often teenagers will ask you to intervene on their behalf, *"Will you talk with Dad about some of the things he says in front of my friends; he totally embarrasses me?"* Be aware of this trap, you are being enticed into becoming the Rescuer. Don't buy into it! This is her problem.

When you step into the role of rescuer, you complete the triangle. If you choose to rescue, then hold on to your hats, the manure is about to hit the fan. When you are the Rescuer, you take on responsibility your teen's problem. You might be a highly skilled and effective Rescuer and get a lot of satisfaction out of it, but you <u>must resist</u> rescuing if you want to empower your teen to solve their problems.

Fun Facts about Adolescents
In her iVillage.com article, Dr. Michele Borba makes 4 points about the value of being honest with your teen.

1. ***Expect honesty.*** *Repeatedly spell out your expectations for honesty:* "Everyone in our family is always expected to be honest with one another." *Once you lay down your honesty expectations, ask your child to promise to tell you the truth (and vice versa).*

2. ***Make it easy for your kid to open up.*** *While you should expect honesty from your kid he also needs to feel safe enough to come to you and admit his mistakes. A* "too harsh" *approach creates fear and he may decide that lying is a better alternative than admitting with the truth; a "too lenient" approach can make lying become a habit he gets away with.*

3. ***Model honesty.*** *One way our kids learn new habits is by modeling our example. So how are you doing? Do you ever:*
   - *Ask your kid to tell the caller you're not home? LIE!*
   - *Keep the change if you're given too much? LIE!*

- *Tell the cashier that your kid is younger to get a break off that ticket price? LIE!*

4. ***Reinforce honesty.*** *Give your kid credit for owning up to his mistakes and having the courage to admit a lie. Behaviors that are reinforced are more likely to be repeated, and repeated behaviors are more likely to become new habits. Praise your child's honesty.*

When Rescuers take action on behalf of the Victim they frequently turn into a Persecutor as they confront the offending party. The original Persecutor feels attacked and takes on the Victim role. In this case Dad has two choices; to seek out a Rescuer (Blames the daughter) or he continue to be the Persecutor with a counter attack on you. Now you have a *Nuclear Chain Reaction.* Is there any wonder why I recommend parents disengage from potential triangulation at all costs? Do not let your teen's problem become yours. Letting your teen have problems is good practice for life.

If you find yourself in a situation where your son or daughter wants you to step into the Rescuer role, be mindful of what you do next. You know when you are about to become a Rescuer. This happens when you are feeling sorry for the "victim." At these times you also have a heightened awareness of the power differential between the Persecutor and the

Victim. These two factors may compel you to jump in and rescue your teen, but . . .

Don't do it!

Engage *Shields Up Scotty*; apply *The Judo Approach* and *Listen to Understand* (Chapter 10). When you rescue, you reinforce your teen's perception that they are powerlessness and you prevent them an opportunity to grow. Below are some other common situations where you might be tempted to jump into your teen's problem.

Your teen comes to you and says,

- *Jacob (younger brother) keeps coming into my room!*
  or
- *I've got so much homework; I don't know where to start!*
  or
- *I hate school!*
  or
- *I'm bored!*
  or
- *I can't stand my math teacher!*
  or
- *Tiffany (her younger sister) keeps wearing my clothes!*
  or
- *I can't believe how old fashioned Mom is! (said to Dad)*
  or

- *I can't believe what Dad did! (said to Mom)*

Your teen's efforts to draw you into solving her problems are evidence that she needs these problems to learn how to handle them. Don't get in her way. Support her resourcefulness and creativity then celebrate her growth as she becomes more skilled at managing her life. Also take note of this; as her critical thinking and problem solving skills improve, the fewer problems she has.

Handy Insight

Problems are opportunities for adolescents to think critically, learn problem-solving skills and begin to trust their judgment.

When you rescue your teenagers you deny them an opportunity for growth and improved self-esteem. In fact, rescuing someone is more about the rescuer's self-esteem than a legitimate desire to help. Pay attention to yourself during these emotionally charged times and make sure you do not get fooled into taking action that your son or daughter needs to take.

The Judo Approach keeps you from falling into the role of Rescuer by accepting what is going on in the moment. It is a reminder to go with the flow of your teen's energy. <u>Do not resist, attach to or judge what is going on around you.</u> Validate their emotional experience and empathize with them. Allow them to burn that energy and get it off their chest. Avoid judging the way they express themselves and do not act on any desire you may have to confront them about their language. They are talking, to you! Be grateful that he or she feels close enough to be telling you this in the first place. *The Judo Approach* connects you with your teen at difficult times in their lives. Never mind that they are over reacting and a little crazy right now. <u>Know</u> that they can handle this problem and express that to them directly. Go ahead, tell them now!

The Judo Approach has another benefit in that it builds trust between you and your teenager. They can trust you to be truthful. Most parents place a high value on honesty, but many parents are not honest with their kids. Honesty means integrity and integrity means rock solid. Isn't this what you want from your teens, honesty and integrity? Remember, the nut doesn't fall too far from the tree.

If you want your children to be honest people, then you, yes YOU, need to be an honest person. When you make a mistake; own up to it. Isn't that what you expect from your kids?

Like *Brain Damaged*, the *Judo Approach* takes very little energy to use. When using *The Judo Approach* you don't get frustrated or angry because <u>you have no conflict and you are emotionally detached from the problem</u>. You have no desire to control your teen's behavior or superimpose your authority on their decision making process. When you acknowledge the validity of your teens perception there is no argument. Like the girl in the mental hospital, the conflict ended immediately because I acknowledged the truth of what she was saying <u>and</u> I took responsibility for myself. She was, after all, correct. I could have made an excuse, but all that would have done is confirm my status as another uncaring adult. Instead, *The Judo Approach* opened up the door for resolution of her conflict with me.

Handy Insight
Adolescents do not have the neurology, the experience, nor the impulse control to respond to their highly emotionally charged state, for lack of a better term, like a grown up.

When you admit your mistake, you take the wind out of your teen's sails, and immediately, you can begin to resolve the problem. *The Judo Approach* also models for your son or daughter how to respond to harsh, and I mean harsh criticism. By the time your teenager has reached the point of dumping this load onto you, they have given hours of thought to the problem but virtual nanoseconds considering what to do about it.

In Chapter 3, I recommended taking some time to re-evaluate your own adolescent experiences. This is also a good time to recall your relationships with your parents. How easy was it for <u>them</u> to admit <u>their</u> mistakes? I'm willing to bet they rarely admitted errors and if they did admit wrongdoing, there was always some reason why it wasn't really their fault. As you recall how your parents responded to you, how did any lack of integrity affect you? Did you lose trust with one or both of your parents? Did you feel betrayed by your parents? What did you need most from your parents at that time? By remembering your own feelings in similar circumstances you are able to <u>empathize</u> with your child.

Please note that simply because your parents made mistakes, these mistakes did not make them bad parents, just as making your own parenting errors does not make you a bad parent. It makes you a human parent. Remember, you are humans raising humans. So do the best you can and if you slip up every once in a while, be OK with it. Simply own it and learn from it. Is it not human to err? I'm sure you tell your kids to do their best and when they fall down, you tell them it's going to be alright? Right? When you make it OK to be OK with mistakes there is no need to defend yourself or make excuses. Forgiveness is a key component of healthy relationships. Start with forgiving yourself first.

The following story represents a typical family in my practice.

Why is it always my fault?

"Tyler" came into therapy at the bequest of his parents. His mother and father explained to me that they were at the end of their rope. Tyler never listened to the; he never followed any of the household rules; he never came home when he was supposed to; he always hung out with the wrong people and he never talked to

them. Essentially, he never did anything right. The parents wanted me to fix Tyler.

At the time, Tyler was 15 years old and he told me that lately he had become "the bad guy" in his family. If anything at all was wrong, according to him, it was automatically his fault. He felt the only way he could deal with this was to stay away from the house as much as possible and when he was at home, he was in his room. He was tired of listening to his parents yell at him and he had decided that as soon as he was old enough, he was going to move out. He knew other kids who were doing just fine on their own—bouncing from one friend's couch to another—and he believed that this would be better than living with people who hated him.

Then one day, in a pivotal family meeting Tyler's mother heard him solemnly say this. She was shocked. She had no idea that he felt so unloved. Tyler's honesty had opened her eyes and as a result of his courage, Tyler's parents were able to express to him how they truly felt. Both, his mother and father told him how much they loved him and how they wanted only the best for him. They were worried about his safety as well as his future and they did not like the distance that had grown between them.

Tyler's father eventually told him about the difficult time he had growing up as an only child in a single parent household after his parents divorced. He told Tyler that he essentially became an orphan because his mother had to work two jobs and his father was so angry with her that he stopped having contact with him and for the most part, disappeared. Tyler's father was devastated and said he felt like he lost both his parents at the same time. He vowed that he would be a better father to his children. Now, he felt like he was failing Tyler. He said, "I know how it feels to lose your parents, son and it must feel like you have lost your mother and I."

With tears in his eyes, Tyler nodded. His father continued and said, "Son, you haven't lost us. We love you. I don't know where this all started going wrong but I want things to be better between us from now on."

Tyler's mother told him much she loved him from the time she knew she was going to have a baby until this very moment. She, too, wanted things to be better between them, and said, "It seems like every time I try to speak with you, I feel like you are shutting me out. I want us to talk without it turning into a yelling match and you storming off to your room, slamming the door behind you. I guess I start to yell when I feel like I am not being heard. Maybe we could change the way we say things to each other."

Because the family was willing to get help, Tyler and his parents took this opportunity to speak honestly and sincerely with each other. The family was able to agree about how and when they would discuss things and where those communications would take place. They also practiced saying things to each other in a gentler way while giving feedback on what they had heard the other person say. They even learned to acknowledge the positive efforts and contributions that everyone was making on a day-to-day basis. Later on, as the family planned some outings they agreed that Tyler could invite one of his friends so his parents could get to know him better. Tyler said "He really is okay, you just don't know him yet!" At that point, the mother softly said to him, "I guess we all need to get to know each other better and I think we have just taken a giant step toward that."

Not all outcomes are as good as this one, but my point is this; at times it pays to get help from a professional family therapist. This family was willing to risk asking for help and with help, each family member was able to make changes in how they communicated, but it was not an instant success. Trust had to be rebuilt among all family members. I needed to have Tyler's trust. Without his trust I would not have been able to create a safe environment and he would not have been able to talk with his parents about his true feelings. Change does not occur overnight, but when families are open to asking for help, results like this can be achieved with a little bit of effort on everyone's part.

Fun Facts about Adolescents

In his 1998 Virginia Polytechnic Institute study "Adolescent Perspectives of Relationship Quality and Daily Interactions with Their Parents," Russell Beazer used a questionnaire to find out what teenagers thought about the quality of their relationships with their parents.

Here are some of his results:

- *86% reported positive interactions with both parents.*

- *85% reported positive interactions with fathers.*

- *80% reported positive interactions with mothers.*

- *88% of Males reported positive interactions with fathers.*

- *63% of Females reported positive interactions with fathers.**

- *86% of Males reported positive interactions with mothers.*

- *89% of Females reported positive interactions with mothers.*

- *25% reported a desire for "more understanding."*

- *25% reported a desire for "more listening."*

- *19% reported a desire for "less time together."*

- *36% reported a desire for "less arguing."*

- *14% reported a desire for "less talking."*

- *14% reported a desire for "more one-on-one time."*

- *22% reported no change desired.*

On average, the adolescents report that the relationships with their parents were important and the overall quality was good.

Although this study is more than a decade old, Russell Beazer's report paints a picture that is recognizable by most teenagers. It is more than a snapshot of the lives of the teenagers he surveyed at that time. It remains true today. This study suggests that most teenagers are satisfied with their family relationships but they also desire some changes at the same time. His study is evidence of the ambivalence that besets adolescence.

Mothers in Beazer's study fared better overall with both sons and daughters, but fathers, according to the survey are struggling with their daughters. In the survey, daughters reported that interactions with their fathers were positive 63% of the time compared to 89% of the time with their mothers. This result is statistically significant and suggests fathers are having difficulty raising their teenaged daughters. Overall, the teenager's views of relationships with both parents were positive; however Beazer's survey suggested that teens, in general do have concerns about their relationships with their parents.

Some of the meaningful changes desired by teens are as follows; over 36% of the respondents had a desire for less arguing and 25% of the teens wanted more understanding from their parents. 25% wanted their parents to be better listeners. Even though 22% of those teens surveyed indicated that there was no need for any changes, it suggests that 78% of those surveyed wanted some change to occur in their families.

Teenagers need to count on their parents. Teens are painfully aware of being dependent on their parents, but they are driven to be autonomous young adults. This is a natural adolescent conflict. It's a conflict between the biological drive to explore the world on their terms and their lifelong dependency upon you. Your adolescent needs to know that you have confidence in them and you will be there if the world gets too difficult for them to handle on their own.

Change is good. Change is growth. Change is constant. Therefore, growth is constant. Imagine what would happen if adolescents didn't change, but remained adolescents forever. Be grateful that the biological drive of all teenagers eventually propels them into *Grownup World*, whether they want to go or not. The challenge for you at this stage of development is to help your teen prepare for this eventuality the best you can. *The Judo Approach* helps you to stay out of their way.

Clear as a Bell

Chapter 9
Clear As a Bell

"Heredity is what sets the parents of a teenager wondering about each other." ~Laurence J. Peter

When you talk with your teen about what you expect from them, be as clear as possible. I suggest you write these expectations down. When your teen fails to meet your expectations talk with them as soon as possible; the sooner the better. *Clear as a Bell* helps you to be clear and precise while at the same time holding your teen accountable. Holding your teen accountable supports their growth and development. Paying attention to what your teen does right super-sizes this tip. It is important to acknowledge and give appreciation when your teen meets or exceeds your expectations. Focusing only on failure is counterproductive and cruel.

Too many parents focus on mistakes. Make sure you address the error, but put more energy into the behavior you want, appreciate and approve of. By doing so, you are supporting their success. Focusing on their failures supports their failure. Do you want them to succeed or do you want them to fail? You make the choice.

Clear as a Bell suggests you use a *matter of fact* approach with your teen. Here are two statements that, when used together, are very effective at letting your teen know what you expect while reminding them that you are there for them. For example:

1. *"I am very concerned about your grades and I expect you to do what it takes to improve them."*

2. *"What do you need from me to do that?"*

This approach lays down the law and offers support at the same time. Teens want and need to be held accountable for their actions, but they also need to feel that you support their efforts.

You may think that your teen understands exactly what you are talking about, but this assumes they have been listening in the first place (which is always a mistake). There is no way that your teenager can understand something as well as you because;

1. you are different people and

2. your teen does not have your experience.

There is another factor adding to this mix. Teenagers view parents and most other adults as *Brain Damaged*. To them, what's the point of listening to you?

Because of this perspective, everything you say to your teen goes through, what I call their *Know It All Filter*. This common adolescent filter reduces your instructions to gibberish. There is no escaping this filter. It surrounds their entire being in all directions and is activated whenever they are in direct contact with adults, especially you. This is one of the reasons you need to be *Clear as a Bell*.

Another factor effecting communications with adolescents is a mechanism that works like a filter in reverse. I call it the *Know It All Amplifier*. It's like a guitar amplifier. The more your teenager is annoyed the louder their *Know It All Amplifier* gets. You will recognize it when your teen says things like;

"Geezz...what do you think I am, an idiot? I know how to do that! Will you leave me alone, for crying out loud?"

At times teenagers will not use words to express their disgust, but will simply turn the volume all the way up and completely drown your voice out. This is often accompanied by one of several classic non-verbal gestures. Don't be distracted by this maneuver. It is simply their way of telling you to buzz off so they can get that chore over with and go back to what they want to do, which, by the way, is not their homework.

Sometimes a teen's *Know It All Filter* and *Know It All Amplifier* are not subtle at all. In fact sometimes they are both turned on full blast at the same time. While working at the Children's Home in Sacramento, CA, I encountered a young teen that had a remarkably simple way of filtering out adult chatter. He had been caught hoarding food in his room, a violation of the rules and upon my approach to talk with him he covered both ears with his hands and began screaming *"la-la-la-la-la-la..."* as loud as he could. I was struck as to how effective this method was. It should be effective; he had both filters going at once.

Granted, this is behavior you might expect from a 4-year-old but not a 14-year-old. However, its bizarre nature was not lost on me. In fact this behavior was an indicator of how developmentally delayed he was when compared with normal adolescents. He continued to hide food in his room which proved how little he trusted others. It also provided valuable insight into how he survived in a family setting where all of his life, he was neglected and abused. These insights lead to a revision in his treatment plan where he was given greater access to food as long as he requested it in an appropriate manner.

Handy Insight
Teenagers learn by doing and

transforming the experience into an understanding of how the world works.

When you give instructions to your adolescent keep in mind that it is more important for them to complete the job than to stand around talking about it. It is essential you understand this. Most teens prefer a minimum of instructions before they set out on a task; even if they have never attempted it before. They are not interested in how you would approach the job, they are more interested in getting it done as fast as possible. That way they can get back to their lives and their friends.

This is an example of how adolescents go about doing things on their own. They want to use their innate knowledge, intuition, and skills. They believe they already know what needs to be done so don't waste your time with lots and lots of instructions. Your teen looks at your requests as an inconvenience and the more details you provide, the more annoyed they will become. You probably already know this, but if you expect them to listen attentively while you go over the details, then you'll be disappointed and frustrated. Your son or daughter's indifference to your directions does not mean what you are saying is not important, it probably is. They simply are not interested. Any effort to pressure them into listening more carefully will further annoy them and activate their filters.

This is because their attention is now focused on ending this discussion and completing the chore as fast as possible or if they can get away with it, not do the chore at all.

From their perspective the time you spend going over the instructions is keeping them from doing the chore (or not). They have better things to do than listen to you go on and on about something they believe is a no brainer. All of this talk gets in the way of returning to their lives.

Don't worry about this; you'll have plenty of time to the discuss details later when you inspect their work. *Inspect their work? What do you mean inspect their work?* I mean, go and inspect their work. This is an opportunity to support your teen in doing a job well done. Your teen may object to an inspection, but pay no attention to their efforts to distract you. If you don't inspect their work, how will you know about the fantastic job they have done. If you don't inspect their work how can you help them do a better job?

Teen World
Versus
Grownup World

Parents and teenagers may live in the same household, but they live in two competing and vastly different worlds. I call these two realities: *Grownup World* and *Teen World*. The differences between these world views are frequently the source of conflict between parents and teenagers. *Teen World* and *Grownup World* are usually on a collision course. When conflict does occur or when these two worlds collide, the cause of the collision is usually a difference in perception. These worlds don't want to crash into each other; they can't help it. How many times have you said to yourself, *"I just don't know what is going on in that kid's head."* or *"Our daughter looked at me like I was out of my mind."*

If your teen. . . .

- listens intently to your every word
- enthusiastically embraces the task at hand
- immediately dives in headfirst
- is focused and determined to meet every standard you have set
- is grateful for the experience
- goes one step further and asks for your opinion on their work
- and asks if there is anything else you would like them to do before they call their friend

Then call the National Security Agency immediately because your teenager has been abducted by a space alien and replaced with an android that looks just like them!

Handy Insight

Your teenager is not interested in what <u>you</u> want them to do. They are interested in what <u>they</u> want to do. It's nothing personal; it is simply the nature of the beast.

You may overestimate at times and misunderstand your teenaged children's interest in *Grownup World*. Most teenagers have a tremendous interest in what's going on in *Teen World*, however, they have very little interest in what is going on in *Grownup World* (unless of course, it directly affects *Teen World*). Well intended, albeit naïve parents make the fatal mistake of assuming their teen is just as interested in *Grownup World* as they are.

Their interest at this stage of development is in what's going on <u>outside</u> of the family, not what is going on <u>inside</u> the family. In *Teen World*, what you are asking them to do is ridiculous and pointless. They really don't understand why you can't see they are busy. For example, your lovely daughter is lying on the couch, dropping potato chips into her mouth from ever increasing heights while watching television. As you approach her, she appears not to notice until you speak. At this point she looks up squinty-eyed and says, in a sharply annoyed tone of voice, *"WHAT?!!"* Dumbstruck and tempted to shout back, you remain calm and say, *"There is something I need you to do."* Pay no attention to the variety of predictable reactions on your daughter's part. Her response to your request is primarily designed to get you to go away and leave her alone as soon as possible. It's nothing personal.

Your daughter may employ her first line of defense by pretending not to hear you. After all, potato chips are <u>really</u> loud! Maybe she didn't hear you. Your once sweet and charming daughter may also try to distract you by saying *"Not now, I'm busy."* She may also say in a high pitched whine, *"Nowwww?!?* Or she may simply roll her eyes and go back to dropping chips into her mouth from arm's length. Do not expect her to stop feeding herself, then sit up and ask you what you'd like her to do. If this is your expectation then you are applying *Grownup World* standards to someone living in *Teen World*. If you make this mistake, there will always be conflict.

Handy Insight

Adolescents are always, and I mean always too busy for adults, even if it appears to the adult that the teen is doing nothing.

Don't take these slights personally. Keep in mind that in *Teen World* the only parents who are higher on the evolutionary scale belong to their friends. And believe me, it is not that much higher. Fortunately, their friends are there to remind them that these people are parents too and therefore, not to be taken seriously. In this way *Teen World* remains stable. Yes, the blind are leading the blind but the good news is; *Teen World* is the perfect place for your son or daughter to live during adolescence.

Let's take a look at how *Teen World* differs from *Grownup World*:

- In *Teen World*, parents and grownups are lower life forms, incapable of rational thought, much less possessing any quality remotely interesting.

- In *Grownup World*, teenagers are lower life forms, incapable of rational thought, much less possessing any quality remotely interesting.

- In *Teen World*, life revolves around friends, other teens, socializing, and freedom. Any time spent with family is wasted and pointless, not to mention potentially embarrassing.

- In *Grownup World*, life revolves around work, family, and responsibility. If there is any time left and if other *Grownup World* friends have any time, then plans might be made to get together. Or go take a nap.

- In *Teen World*, the goal of day-to-day life is to get away from *Grownup World* and ignore *Sibling World*. An exception may occur if *Teen World* perceives there is something to be gained by interacting with *Grownup World*. When *Teen World* sees something to be gained, it seizes the opportunity! *Teen World* can be amazingly helpful at these times.

- In *Grownup World*, the goal of day-to-day life is to provide for the needs of *Teen World*, work and toil out in the *Real World* and make personal sacrifices while at the same time remaining sane.

- In *Teen World* life means freedom, liberty, and eternal life.

- In *Grownup World* life means working hard, saving money, retiring and then dying.

- In *Teen World* everything is happening in the moment. Life is a series of urgent and important events that need immediate attention.

- In *Grownup World*, everything is painstakingly detailed and requires precise planning and execution.

As you can see from these examples there is a vast difference between *Teen World* and *Grownup World*. If you worry that your son or daughter won't make it to *Grownup World* if they keep doing what they are doing, then you are normal. You may have heard yourself or a friend say, *"I'm not sure if Jessica is going to graduate, she doesn't seem to care about school. I don't know what she's going to do. It's like she doesn't want to grow up."*

Don't worry about your teen growing up; they don't have a choice. Eventually everyone becomes an adult, but as you know, some adults are more grownup than others. Your teen is acutely aware that someday he or she will need to leave *Teen World*. They are also aware of their need to learn how to live in *Grownup World*. This powerful biological drive cannot be denied. Diverted yes, but not denied. Your job is to maximize your teen's potential. *Clear as a*

Bell is another tool that helps you meet that challenge.

Teenagers need to try out their ideas in the real world. This includes their idea of when a chore needs to be completed. Don't be discouraged when your son or daughter fails to meet your time expectations. Instead, rejoice, this is an opportunity to use *Clear as a Bell* and at the same time help them to listen better when receiving instructions. In this way, the next time you ask them to do something, there is less confusion.

Handy Insight

Make sure your teen takes responsibility for any task they are capable of doing and <u>need</u> to do for themselves. This teaches self-reliance.

Clear as a Bell's secret weapon is an under-the-radar, stealth missile called O*wning Your Own*. This means you, the parent, take responsibility for *not* being clear in the directions you gave in the first place. Yes, you heard me. Just do it. I know you believe you were very clear, but certain details were lost in the translation from *Adult World* to *Teen World*. *Owning Your Own* sounds something like this:

"I noticed you didn't get that job done that I asked you to do this morning. I'm sorry, I may not have been clear about when I wanted it finished."

Owning Your Own takes your teen by surprise. This is the farthest thing from their minds. They might silently stare at you, like a deer caught in the headlights of a car. It's almost impossible for them to imagine you are not blaming them for screwing up. *"What do you mean it's your fault?"* says your son. Teenagers never expect this from adults, especially their parents. When applied successfully, over time your teenager learns not to filter out the content of your instructions. They are less inclined to turn on their filters and they do a better job. By *Owning Your Own*, you share the problem with your teenager. They expect you to criticize their work. In *Teen World* this means you are trying to keep them from doing what they want to do; which is oftentimes, nothing.

Fun Facts about Adolescents

In their article, "Gaining Freedom: Self-Responsibility in Adolescents with Diabetes" published in Pediatric Nursing, Becky J. Christian, Jennifer P. D'Auria, Leslie C. Fox discuss the following: "Several different aspects of experiential learning were identified as being important to the achievement of independence in early to mid-adolescence. These included the need to:

- *gain ongoing factual knowledge*
- *be allowed to make choices*

- *have opportunities to validate choices*

- *practice complex decision making*

- *spend periods of time away from their family to practice new skills.*

All of these experiences were identified as being necessary to build confidence in becoming more independent from parents."

Adolescents are generally on high alert and have their fingers on the buttons that operates another filter called the B*lah, Blah, Blah filter.* Often this filter gets activated along with the amplifier in an effort to render any criticism of their work completely ineffective.

If you combine *Clear as a Bell* with *Two Little Words* for instance, you increase dramatically the likelihood that your teen will learn from the experience. Here's an example:

You've asked your teen to clean the kitchen after dinner (a task they are well equipped to do) and you spew out a set of expectations like: do the dishes, wipe down the table and countertops, take out the garbage and sweep the floor. In *Grownup World* this is not rocket science, but in *Teen World*, all of this talk is annoying and a waste of time. What's the point? The kitchen is just going to get dirty again tomorrow, why does it constantly need to be cleaned? Begrudgingly, they head into the kitchen and return a few minutes later announcing, *"I'm finished."*

Ah, the moment of truth! They lead you into the kitchen where you notice that the dishes are done, the table and countertops are wiped down and clear. There are still some remnants of dinner under the table but the rest of the floor has been swept. <u>The first thing you do is comment on how nice the table and countertops look and how pleased you are by the way they loaded the dishwasher.</u> By focusing on what your son or daughter did well; you hit them with another secret weapon called the *AttaBoy or AttaGirl.* In closing this scene, you say to you daughter, *"I'm sorry, I should have asked you to sweep under the table. How silly of me. What do you see there?"* At which time your teen may get the broom, mumble a few things under their breath and sweep up the scraps. This is a wonderful time to say *"Thank you; I really appreciate your help."* Had you immediately focused on the scraps under the table her <u>good</u> work would have been lost in the shadow of criticism.

Again, if your teen does not meet your expectations, *Clear as a Bell* suggests you immediately assume responsibility for not being clear with them. This puts your teen off balance and they cannot engage their filters nor can they turn up their amplifier. Explain to them how you could have done a better job of communicating. Perhaps writing the instructions down might have been more helpful. Thank them for the good work and show them how much you appreciate their efforts. When you are *Clear as a Bell* there is less likelihood that your teen will object to helping around the house and when you focus on what they are doing well they may even surprise you with a desire to do an extra good job.

Handy Insight

Avoid asking Yes or No questions. Using open ended questions gets more information and more cooperation from your teen.

Clear as a Bell works for your teen as well. How many times has your teen complained *"You don't understand"* and they are right! You don't understand. It is just as important for them to be *Clear as a Bell* when asking you to do something as it is for you to be clear. Of course, this makes no sense to teenagers. In their mind they think, *"I've just told you what I wanted, why don't you understand?"* They know perfectly well what they need and you, being the adult, should know precisely what they are talking about. Right? Right.

This is tricky territory because your teen will not automatically know how to be *Clear as a Bell*; therefore it requires a great deal of patience on your part. A most effective way to help them learn this valuable communication skill is to ask questions such as, *"What do you mean?"* or *"What exactly do you need?"* That's right, take advantage of being *Brain Damaged.* At first your teen may become annoyed or irritated with you but pay no attention to this. The point is to gather as many details as soon as possible. You know what will happen if <u>you</u> make a mistake or forget something. Forget about any *AttaBoys* too.

The more information you get, the better you can follow through. For example, your son comes to you and says, *"I need a ride."* Never mind the fact that you are in the middle of cooking dinner. Being the good enough parent that you are, you stop what you are doing and ask; *"Where do you want to go?"*

- He says, *"My friend's house."*

- You say, *"OK, which friend?"*

- He says, *"Johnny,"* slightly irritated.

- You say, *"Which Johnny?"* (He has two friends named Johnny)

- He says, *"Johnny Kapillary, geez...!"*

- You say, *"What time do you want to go?"*

- He says, *"Right now! What are you doing? Can you take me?"*

- You say, *"What are you going to do at Johnny's?"*

- He says, *"Mom......!?!"*

- You say, *"What about your homework?"*

- He says, *"I've done it."*

- You say, *"What about your chores?"*

- He says, *"Done them too."*

- You say, *"What do Johnny's parents say about you coming over?"*

- He says, *"It's OK with them, for crying out loud, can you take me or not?"*

As difficult as this line of questioning is for you, it is doubly difficult for your teen. Adolescents are not interested in details. What's important to them is getting what they want as soon as possible. However, it is absolutely necessary to ask questions if you are going to understand what they need. Patience and persistence are keys to super sizing *Clear as a Bell*.

Handy Insight

Ever notice that the only time your teenager needs you is when you're right in the middle of doing something?

It's true that residents of *Teen World* can communicate telepathically with each other, but for those of us in *Grownup World* depend upon a basic form of communication; speech and the use of words to share information and ideas. Try to appreciate the irony when you attempt to extract relevant information from your adolescent. This leads me to yet another formula.

$$\#T + T > \#T + G$$

Where:

\# = Number of Words

T = Teenager
and
G = Grownup

In other words:
The number of words adolescents use with teenagers is ALWAYS greater than the number of words adolescents use with adults.

This formula compares how many words teenagers use when talking with other teens and how many words they use when talking with adults. You may experience this every day in your own home. Haven't you noticed there is a lot of talking going on when your teen is on the phone with a friend? Plus, it sounds like both of them are talking at the same time! (more evidence that teenagers must have some sort of telepathic power.) Have you ever been at school when the class bell has sounded? You need earplugs to keep from going deaf. All of the students are talking as fast as they can and as loud as they can. It is amazing how many words get exchanged among teenagers between classes.

Now imagine all of you are sitting at the dinner table and you can hear a pin drop. Breaking the silence, you ask your daughter, with as much curiosity as you can muster, *"How was school today?"* *"Fine"* she says. Does this sound familiar? Some parents might respond to the absence of detail by playing *20 Questions* with mixed results at best. A good thing to say in this situation is,

"That's nice, let us know if anything interesting happened today. I would love to hear about it."

This lets your teen know that you are interested and allows them the time and space to share *Teen World* at their discretion and not at your beck and call. Immediately move on to another conversation with a different family member. Teens often have mixed feelings about sharing *Teen World* with their family. By creating a strong relationship with your teen they are more than willing to share the events of their day. This makes for a wonderful dinner experience.

The boy in the previous example wanted to go to his friend's house as soon as possible. This means he was motivated to do what it takes to accomplish this goal. His desire to go to his friend's was strong enough to tolerate the questions. It may have been annoying for him, but it is well worth the effort.

On the other hand, your daughter did not have the need to talk about her day. It was your need. Who knows how her day was? Only she knows and she's not sharing, at least not now.

Even a benign question like *"How was your day?"* can feel highly intrusive to teenagers. Pay attention when you ask this question and you may see them shrinking, just a little, into their chair. By responding to your daughter with interest and not prodding, you allow her be where she is and at the same time let her know that you are interested in her life. It opens up what I call a <u>safe space</u> for her to talk about her day, when she is ready. Your teen's monosyllabic responses are not necessarily an effort to withhold information, although that is definitely a possibility. Most responses like this are part of teenager's efforts to manage and control their domain. Don't take it personally.

Handy Insight

Seek a balance of communication among all family members.

The next time you and your teen are talking pay attention to how much you are speaking and how much they are speaking. If you are talking more than they are then you run the risk of cutting off communication. Strive for a balance of communication with all family members and if they are not sharing with you then you might be talking too much. If you think you are talking too much, you probably are. Use *Clear as a Bell* to stop yourself. Relax, take a deep breath. Then ask an open ended question like, *"What do you hear me saying?"* Or better yet; *"Well look at me, I'm talking a mile a minute."* I know you have many concerns for your teen and you are doing your best to keep the conversation going. However, parents who use more than 50% of the words when talking with their teen are interfering with their teen's ability to contribute to the conversation. Think about it. If your teen is not sharing, maybe it's because they can't get a word in edgewise. Dominating conversations may indicate a problem with anxiety.

Fun Facts about Adolescents

Beth A Le Poire, in her book, "Family Communication: Nurturing and Control in a Changing World, discusses the following regarding the adolescents changing view of the family. "Regardless of these differences in perception of the adolescent-parent relationship, parents should rest assured that their communication with their adolescents is important. Specifically, parent-adolescent relationships are the most influential in important adolescent decisions (Collins, Maccoby, Steinberg, Hetherington, and Bornstein, 2000). In addition, positive communication between parents and adolescents can be related to positive outcomes for the adolescents. Adolescents who view their communication with their parents as positive report greater positive feelings of self-worth, enhanced well-being and better coping behaviors (Buri, Kirchner & Walsh, 1987; Jackson, Bijstra, Oostra, & Bosma, 1998; Lanze, Iafrante, Rosnati, & Scabini, 1999).

As the parent of a teenager you may find yourself talking too much quite frequently and you may even feel strongly about what you are saying. But before you know it, your teen goes into a trance or accuses you of lecturing them. A hyper-verbal response can also occur when you are worried, anxious or angry with your teen. When you are filled with strong emotions and go on and on and on....you leave little room for your teen to say anything. Now this may feel good to you, but it feels really bad for your kid.

If this sounds like you at times, keep in mind that the main reason for your verbosity is your need to be heard. After all it's your job to educate them about life, to teach them critical skills and give them valuable insights. Certainly, your accumulated wisdom can help your teen get through this difficult time. If only they would listen.

Handy Insight

Just because your teenager is not talking doesn't mean they are listening.

Teenagers can develop strong feelings of shame and low self-esteem if they believe their home is dominated by constant lecturing. There must be room in the conversation for them to share. Under these conditions communication breaks down and an ever widening gulf develops, creating a sense of alienation and isolation within your adolescent.

Clear as a Bell is about quality and not quantity. Remember, when you find yourself going on and on while your teen's eyes slowly glaze over, remind yourself that communication is a two-way street. Don't be a road hog! Always strive for balance and harmony in your communications with your teens as well as everyone else.

Chapter 10
Listen to Understand

Telling a teenager the facts of life is like giving a fish a bath. ~Arnold H. Glasow

Once your adolescent starts talking to you, listening becomes the <u>most effective</u> tip for taming teenagers. If you are going use *Listen to Understand* effectively, you must be prepared to hear things you don't want to hear. You must encourage your teen to express themself in their own words, even if you don't like the way they say it. Do not censure them in any way, shape or form. This takes longer, but with your handy *Teen World/Grownup World* dictionary you will soon understand what they are talking about. Adolescents have an overwhelming need to be heard, especially by you, even though you are *Brain Damaged.* When you *Listen to Understand*, it means that you listen without forming judgments, offering solutions, or stating opinions about what you hear. By listening intently, you open the door to understanding, acceptance, and trust. Use this tip in combination with all of the other tips and triple their power.

I know, at times your teen has accused you of *"ruining"* their life or *"embarrassing them to death",* but these accusations are natural stepping stones towards separation and individuation. They need to know that you will

215

listen to them, no matter how badly they express themselves. When you *Listen to Understand* it is the best way to tell your teen that their opinions matter to you. Soon, they will be asking for your advice. Look! Is that a flying pig?

These guidelines are simple because they need to be. Simple works! Plus, simple makes *Ten Tips to Tame Your Teen* easy to remember. This makes it easy for you to consistently use this information. It's not necessary to talk about all of that developmental mumbo jumbo. Make communication with your teenager simple and soon <u>you</u> will not be able to get a word in edgewise.

Avoid imposing these guidelines on anyone else in your family. Attempts to do so will trigger resistance on their part. Talking to your teenager about these guidelines will set off alarms in their heads, activating their filters, which will render anything you say henceforth futile. The Ten Tips are great ideas to put into practice for yourself and by doing so you will improve the quality of communication with your teen. Using *Ten Tips to Tame Your Teen* every day improves the communication with your teen and your entire family. Eventually other family members may become interested. Meanwhile, enjoy the moment.

You may not know how to begin to listen effectively so I have compiled a list of *20 Questions* for you to practice with. These questions are designed to keep the lines of communication open and help you to <u>follow</u> the conversation as opposed to <u>leading</u> or <u>directing</u> the conversation. It is important to know that you are not a detective solving a crime and you are not a reporter getting the facts for your story. You are a parent and you love your teenager, but based upon their behavior, they're having problems. If you try to get to the bottom of this unknown problem, you will end up <u>leading</u> the conversation. The minute your teen senses your tractor beam dragging them into your investigation, their filters are activated. You can't fool them; they know you are more interested in making your point than listening to them.

Your adolescent can also feel the tug from questions that start with W, you know, Who? What? Where? Why? When? I call these the 5 W's and asking these questions reflects <u>your</u> need to know. Questions along this line also activate your teen's filters.

"W" questions take your teen away from where they need to be. Besides, they're not interested in solving the problem right now anyway. They just want to talk. What your teen needs now is for you to listen. The "W" questions also take your teen away from their feelings. You want them to feel their emotions as well as express them. You don't want to shut that down. The 5 W's are appropriate later on after the emotional turmoil has subsided, but not until then.

Imagine your son or daughter has just arrived home. They run into the house, slam the front door, then run to their room cursing and slamming their bedroom door. (Oh yeah, and they are late too!)

1. What are you thinking right now?
2. What are you feeling right now?
3. What are you compelled to do right now?

Whatever that is don't do it. Wait.

There is always a reason for behavior. If your teenager was ready to talk, they would walk right up and tell you. They would interrupt you before you could have even considered the above questions.

By slamming two doors, cursing, and going straight to their room, your teen is communicating two very important things:

1. There is a problem
and
2. They are *not* ready to talk about it

Respect this communication and if you need to take a few deep breaths, then do so, but right now <u>do nothing</u>. Yes I know you want to bolt from your chair, pound on their bedroom door and demand to come in. This is not the time to deal with all of the cursing and door slamming. That can wait. Give them 15-20 minutes of alone time. Any less time and you are intruding; any more than 15-20 minutes and they begin to wonder if you still care about them. Go figure. If you think it is difficult being a parent of an adolescent; imagine what it's like for an adolescent to be *your* teenager!

When you eventually decide to venture to their room, unlike *The Hit and Run*, you have no point to make and you have no prepared statement. You are there to *Listen to Understand.* Before you knock on their door, activate *Shields Up Scotty.* Be prepared to use *The Judo Approach* as well as *What? Me Worry?* but most of all, be cool, calm, collected and supportive.

The *20 Questions* below are helpful when you need to support your child during highly emotional times, like most days. The *20 Questions* also help you to <u>follow</u> the conversation and therefore you can *Listen to Understand* effectively. There no specific order to the *20 Questions* but it <u>is</u> important to ask the right question at the right time. When you do, it leads to more sharing. However, if you ask the right question at the wrong time you run the risk of shutting down the conversation. Asking the wrong question at the wrong time will result in your expulsion from their room. Nevertheless, don't worry too much about what question to ask. If you are following the conversation, your teen will clue you in as to what question is next.

Listen to Understand means waiting for the appropriate time and then asking the question that is most likely to validate their experience and encourage them to continue talking. So, here they are.......... *The 20 Questions*!

1. Wow, you're really upset!

2. Really?

3. What was that like?

4. Then what happened?

5. What else can you tell me?

6. What's going on for you right now?

7. How do you feel about them now? (Teen problems usually involve other teens.)

8. How do you feel about your reaction?

9. What do you think they were feeling?

10. I don't understand, would you repeat that, please?

11. What would you like to have happen?

12. What would you like to do about this?

13. What can you do about this?

14. Who else have you talked to?

15. What was their reaction?

16. How do you feel about their reaction?

17. Who else would you like to talk to?

18. How do you think this happened?

19. What part, if any, do you think you have in this problem?

20. What are you thinking right now?

21. What are you feeling right now?

22. What do you need from me?

23. How can I help?

24. Say "Yes" or "Uh huh" while nodding your head.

25. Who can help you with this?

26. How are you taking care of yourself?

27. It's OK

28. Everything will be alright.

29. I love you.

OK, you're right, there are more than *20 Questions* AND they are not all questions. There are even a few W questions stuck in there, too! Nevertheless, try using these along with any of your own wonderful questions that pop up at the moment. Trust your gut. The *20 Questions* open the door to understanding and at the same time helps your teen assume responsibility for themselves.

The more you use the *20 Questions* the more information you get from your teen and the better they feel about solving their own problems. They also feel closer to you because you have demonstrated you care about them, and you are willing to stand by and listen while they figure it out themselves.

Fun Facts about Adolescents

In her article "Communicating with Your Teen," Shannon L. Sachs, working with Ohio State University, has created guidelines for effective communication with your teenaged children. She suggests there are ten factors involved in communicating with your adolescent.

1. *Learn something new from the speaker.*

2. *Stay focused on the other person.*

3. *Be an active listener.*

4. *Match the speaker's emotional state, unless it is hostile.*

5. *Withhold advice unless asked to give it.*

6. *Draw a mental picture of what the other person is saying.*

7. *Put yourself in the other person's shoes.*

8. *Think before you speak.*

9. *Encourage the other person.*

10. *Be pleasant.*

Try using these active listening skills with your adolescent. After some practice, introduce your family to the idea of using effective communication skills. Describe the guidelines presented here, and take turns being the listener. See the difference that good communication skills can make in your family!

It is critical to your teen's growth and development they understands their responsibility in the relationships of their lives. Do not, however, make this the first thing you talk about. Keep it in the back of your mind, trust your gut, and use your empathy skills to know when to address their responsibility. Be patient and do the crisis work first.

Handy Insight

Teenagers do want to take responsibility for their lives, no matter what they do or say to the contrary.

As you listen to your teen tell their side of the story, match their affect, like you are their reflection in a mirror. In this way, when they look at you they see the concern in your face that's in their heart. By matching or mirroring their affect you connect with your teen on a nonverbal level. This tells them you understand how they feel.

I know your teen is really upset and as much as you want them to regain their composure, it is important to let them be, so continue to be patient and supportive. They have their own process which is likely to be quite different than yours. Their emotions are the stuff of growth and allowing them to sit with these feelings will do them no harm and will benefit them greatly.

Regardless of the problem your child has, it is important to impress upon them that you care about what they are saying. <u>You cannot fake this!</u> Stay focused on them. They know you well and the second you become distracted, they are on to you. As much as you may want to wrap it up, any attempt to rush the process will be interpreted by your teen as disinterest. This says other things are more important than listening to them. That's not a message you want to send. Here are a few things you can do to ensure that they know you are interested in hearing about their problem.

- Assume the listening position (Sit down, face your teen and look directly into their eyes, then lean forward resting your forearms on your thighs.)
- Express concern with your eyes
- Don't say anything until it is appropriate

- Do not interrupt or correct their language
- Use one of the *20 Questions* if appropriate
- Wait for their response
- Let silence work for you
- Use another one of the *20 Questions*
- Keep following their lead
- Base the next question on their last response

Repeat as necessary.

Don't let your mind wander and be sure to stay focused on their painful saga. Resist the urge to look at your watch and be grateful they are talking with you all, much less pouring their heart out. You are doing a wonderful thing for your kid when you *Listen to Understand*. Once the seas have calmed, you can begin to explore how they may have contributed to the problem. No, you are not going to let them off the hook and it's OK to ask . . .

"What do you think your part is in this problem?"

Take note of any attempt to deny responsibility, but do not comment. Continue to us the *20 Questions* to understand how *they* see the problem. A good 1-2 combination at these times is to say;

Ten Tips to Tame Your Teen

1. *Really?*
2. *Tell me more about that.*

Should your adolescent become defensive and deny any responsibility it is evidence that they are not ready to accept their role in the problem. As long as your teen believes they are a victim they will not be able to see their part. The good news is this; adolescence is the perfect time to teach them the power of *Owning Their Own*. Adolescence is also a good time for them to practice *Owning Their Own* thoughts, *Owning Their Own* feelings, and *Owning Their Own* decisions. When you *Listen to Understand,* like *The Judo Approach,* you facilitate this process without torturing them with lectures and stories with morals attached to them.

If your teen is unable to stop feeling like a victim, you may need to back off a bit and wait until they run their head into that wall again. Perhaps they need to talk with a friend, write in a journal or see a counselor. If and when you feel like you're not getting anywhere, then back off and make a clean getaway. Privacy may be what your teen needs right now. Let them know that you will check in with them later and gracefully leave them alone. Remember, unless it is a life or death situation or there is clear and present danger, then most things can wait.

By allowing your teen to feel their emotions for as long as they need to, you help them grow from the experience and they are better prepared the next time they encounter a similar situation. When people have the experience of another person taking the time to listen without judging or attempting to solve the problem, it strengthens the bond between them. *Listen to Understand* increases the intimacy, trust, and love between you and your teen. It is, by far, the most powerful tip in this book.

Listen to Understand is so powerful that I make my living by *Listening to Understand*. Parents pay me to listen to their kids. Imagine that! When I tell people I have worked with adolescents for over 40 years they are most amazed that anyone could or would do something like that. This always surprises me because I have benefited as much from listening to them as they have benefited from me listening.

Eventually, these kids ask, *"What do I do now?"* Since I know it is not my job to tell them what to do I am able to pass the problem back to them, *"What do you want to do?"* This supports their problem solving process <u>and</u> uses their brain. Remember, like you, I'm also *Brain Damaged*, but it's my job to follow their process and support those ideas that are most likely to succeed. For those ideas that are a bit off the wall or poorly thought out, I used the *20 Questions*.

Handy Insight

If your teenager denies responsibility for circumstances that are clearly a result of their choices, it's a sign that they are more fragile than they appear.

When you use the *20 Questions* the message you send to your teen is you trust them to create a viable solution to the problem. Using the *20 Questions* helps your adolescent to develop critical thinking and problem solving skills. They become more aware of their feelings, the feelings of others and they learn how to consider the possible outcomes before taking action. Over time, *Listen to Understand* reduces your teen's tendency for impulsivity and reactivity to people and events in their lives.

Most adults have a lot of experience and make these decisions automatically without much thought. On the other hand, teenagers, automatically and without much thought, put most events into the <u>Urgent and Important</u> category. Although, this may appear to be counterproductive, which it is, any attempt to *"help"* your teen see they are overreacting will result in denial and resistance on their part. For example, how often do they calm down when you tell them to calm down? I thought so. Helping your teen in this way is an attempt to <u>lead</u> the conversation, thereby proving to them that you really don't care and you don't trust their judgment. Hang in there and in time they will get better at prioritizing their life. In the meantime trust their innate ability to learn from these experiences.

Most events in our lives fall into one of the 4 categories in the table below.

Urgent And Important	Not Urgent But Important
Urgent But Not Important	Not Urgent And Not Important

To you, their troubles may seem trivial and insignificant, but at this moment these problems are the most important issues in their young lives. In this helter-skelter world, they are at the mercy of the adults around them and the institutions they have to be part of. Their problems are no less significant than yours. The biggest difference is they have virtually no experience in solving problems. This lack of experience contributes to their daily drama.

If your teenager is overreacting to an event use *The 0-10 Scale*. Ask your teen how much the problem is impacting them using a 0-10 scale where 0 means the problem has no impact and 10 means the problem has the biggest impact ever. It matters not what their answer is because the next question is this; *"What does that mean to you?"* or *"What's that like for you to be an 8 or a 10 or a 2?"* In order to fully understand your son's or daughter's perspective you need to know how they interpret their experiences. *Listen to Understand* helps you to see the world through their eyes.

It is helpful to ask your teen what they would say to a friend who is having the same problem. Teenagers love to be of service to their friends and this is a good way for them to explore possible outcomes by pretending they are helping a friend. After all, how many times have you watched your teen drop everything when a friend is in need? When you use this hypothetical situation you discover that your kid has a pretty good head on their shoulders. I know, why can't they move with the same urgency when the garbage needs to be taken out or their room needs to be cleaned?

Try role playing with your teen. It's fun and it helps them see the problem from a different perspective. Role playing also helps your teen to become more empathetic. By role playing you get to see how they respond to a friend they care about. Role plays help them to practice the action they are planning to take. When you are in the role of their friend or your teen (yes you get to play your teen too) use your imagination and bring a sense of urgency and realism to this make-believe situation. Role playing helps your teen see themselves through your role play of them and they get some practice with the action they want to take. This leads to a greater capacity for empathy and a stronger self-image.

The great thing happens when you *Listen to Understand;* you get to know your son or daughter. You become privy to their private thoughts and feelings. You get to know their true selves and how they create meaning in their lives. You get to be that fly on the wall, the trusted adult to whom they reveal the most intimate details of their world and how they interpret the events in their life. *Listen to Understand* and they won't need me.

Take a moment or two and look back at how you dealt with problems when you were a teenager. What's similar? What's different? At those times, it is helpful to tell your teen one of your life stories when you were feeling the same way. When you disclose personal history, it says, *"I got through it and I know you will too."* Don't be a stranger to your kids.

Being an adolescent is exhausting. *Teen World* is filled with urgent and important decisions that need to be made on a day-to-day and moment-to-moment basis. All teenagers experience life as a series of urgent and important events happening one right after the other. Is it any wonder why they eat and sleep so much?

Many parents I work with are impatient with their kids. They want their kids to get through adolescence as fast as possible. The vast majority of these parents are well meaning and good enough parents. Unfortunately, due to many failed and exhausting efforts, they are unable to see anything positive about their teen. *Listen to Understand* takes time. It requires you to focus and it tests your patience. I learned many years ago that I cannot <u>push the river</u>. The same is true for adolescent development. They are not going to grow up any faster than they do.

These well-meaning parents pride themselves on being cool, calm and collected professionals but feel frustrated and confused each time they watch their teenager ignore their best efforts to parent them. They've lectured, they've cajoled and they've commanded their teens. At times they may have even said, *"It's my way or the highway!"* This is when they come to see me. By the time a family enters counseling, the communication is virtually non-existent and their kids spend as much time away from home as possible. These cases are challenging because of the tremendous animosity that has accumulated over the years. What helped these parents more than anything was to learn how to *Listen to Understand.*

Many of these parents felt as though they had failed their children while others blamed their teens for all of the family problems. When working with these families, it is important to reestablish the boundaries and redefine who is responsible for what. Then the vacuum of communication needs to be filled with supportive and positive verbal exchanges. Therefore I require families to pay attention and comment on their teen's positive actions in positive ways.

One of the exercises I do with families is called *Positive Bombardment.* In this exercise, one family member at a time is targeted with a positive comment from the other family members, one at a time. The bombarded person is only allowed to say *"Thank you"* or *"You're welcome."* One by one, each family member gets bombarded with positive comments until everyone in the family has been bombarded. Then we talk about what this experience was like for each of them.

This is a very powerful exercise and if you decide to give it a go in your family you may get some surprising results. Granted, your situation may not be as dire as some of the families I work with, but I encourage you to have a family meeting anyway, if only to do this exercise. Have fun with it. Afterwards everyone feels better about themselves and their relationships with each other. What do you have to lose? Be aware that your teen may attempt to sabotage anything good about this exercise.

Handy Insight

Pay attention to the behavior you like. Positively reinforce positive behavior! Say something nice. The plant that survives and grows is the one that gets sunshine and water. When you notice what your teen does right it is like watering and feeding your plants or opening the door when your dog or cat needs to go out. They like it.

As a follow-up to the *Positive Bombardment* exercise, I challenge families to say something positive to every other family member <u>three times a day</u>. Yes, I want you to practice being nice to each other at least <u>three</u>

times every day. You should see some of the parents squirm when they are asked to make 3 positive comments to every family member every day, including themselves. Often a family would try to negotiate a lower number, like once a day or twice a week. Many family members would exclaim, *"I can't do that!"* or *"What if there's nothing positive to say?"* or *"I don't really want to talk with these people much less make up something nice to say to them."* I tell them to just do it and see what happens.

If your teen rejects this feedback and they become argumentative and angry, do not despair because eventually, even the most guarded and hostile of teens will respond to being acknowledged for who they are and what they do right. At the moment, low self-esteem is not permitting them to accept these *AttaBoys*, but over time, their self-esteem improves. Keep on making these positive comments and you will begin to see all kinds of wonderful things to be positive about.

When you *Listen to Understand*, you are doing just as much for your teen as providing for their physical needs. This tip reinforces the very behavior you want your teen to manifest. *Listen to Understand* not only positively reinforces your adolescent's positive behavior, it reinforces their sense of well-being, their connectedness with others and their ability to function in the world at large. Make liberal use of this tip on a daily basis, then sit back, relax and watch your teen grow into that totally awesome adult.

After Word

Ten Tips to Tame Your Teen

After Word

Now that you have read *Ten Tips to Tame Your Teen* it is time to get out there and put it to good use. Start practicing these tips and little by little you will get the hang of them. Soon, they will become as natural as grinding your teeth used to be. As mentioned in the Introduction, read this book again, only this time highlight anything that you think is important for you to remember. After you have read this book a second time and highlighted all of the important stuff, read it again, only this time only the material you have highlighted. If your eyes wander into the un-highlighted text, that's alright. It doesn't hurt to review those parts either.

By reading *Ten Tips to Tame Your Teen* again and again you hone your skills with the tools in this book? When you are intimately familiar with the Ten Tips you ensure your success. When you respond to your teen differently they will respond differently to you. Pay attention to these positive changes. Comment on them. Bring them up at dinner time or in the car when you are driving your teen to the mall. You bought this book because you were serious about helping your teen. You read this book because you found the approaches simple to understand and easy to do. You will integrate these tips into your family life because you love your kids and you want to have healthy and loving relationships with them throughout your lives.

237

Thank you for getting this far in your pursuit of a better relationship with your teenager. The changes you make will bring this new reality to you and your family. It is time to trust yourself, trust your ability to use Ten Tips effectively and most of all it is time to believe in your teen.

You are the reason I wrote this book and my only regret is that I did not complete it sooner. My sole desire is to help as many teenagers and families as possible. I know that raising teenagers is challenging, but your life does not need to be a pit of drama even though it might be for your teen. Raising teenagers does not need to be a constant power struggle. It does not need to be difficult or painful. After all, your only job as a parent is to prepare them for the world. A piece of cake, right? Right. Even though raising teenagers is serious business, *Ten Tips to Tame Your Teen* is here to remind you that you cannot take this responsibility too seriously otherwise you squeeze all of the fun out of your family.

Believe your teen is capable and competent then behave accordingly with them. Soon, you will see that shining star. The one that you know, in your heart, is there. May your lives be blessed with lifelong loving relationships that are filled with abundance and joy. Thank you for all you are doing to make this world a better place.

Ray   Erickson

About the Author

"Change your mind and change your life."
- Ray Erickson

Dear Reader,

After more than 30 years of working with teenagers and their families I have come to the conclusion that all of us, in one way or another are recovering adolescents. *Ten Tips to Tame Your Teen* is my attempt to help you create a more rewarding, more meaningful and a more joyful relationship with your adolescent children.

I have either been an adolescent or I've worked with adolescents. I was only 19 years-old when I took on my first adult role with teenagers. I was a sophomore in college and returned to my former high school on a 6-week student teaching assignment. At that time, my idea of a perfect teacher was my old high school physics teacher. His name was Mr. Fred Gore. He was a hulking hulk of a man and frequently referred to himself as Mr. God and I believed him. All of the students were afraid of him even though he never did anything to threaten or intimidate; he simply had a commanding presence. At 19, I was not a hulking hulk and I didn't even come close to being Mr. God. And if that wasn't enough, Mr. Gore was teaching in the very next room. Needless to say, I was a poor Mr. Gore, but nevertheless, I went on to earn bachelor degrees in Mathematics and Sociology from Western Michigan University. I then taught junior and senior high school until 1981 when I left teaching defeated and discouraged. Teaching was extremely difficult for me. I was not a very good teacher. However, what remained deep within me was a commitment to help young people to the best of my ability, one way or another.

Then in the early 1980s while living in Boise, Idaho I applied for a teaching position in a psychiatric hospital. I was turned down for that job but was offered another position as a psychiatric technician. My new job was to hang out with the kids, talk with them and take them on outings in the community. I loved it. I loved working with these *"troubled"* youth. I couldn't believe I was getting paid. In those days, teenagers were routinely hospitalized for months at a time, so I really got to know them. You rarely see that nowadays, which is a good thing. If I had been hired as a teacher I would not have discovered another way to work with teenagers.

In 1984 I moved to Sacramento, CA to pursue a Master of Social Work degree. While attending California State University I worked at the Sacramento Children's Home and did two internships in residential treatment facilities. My experiences in Idaho thrust my career into the world of severely emotionally disturbed adolescents (SED). I've worked with abused, neglected and abandoned teenagers ever since then. I've also worked with adolescent sex offenders in outpatient clinics and residential treatment centers. In my private practice I work with kids just like yours who are stressed out, anxious or depressed just dealing with life.

In my career I've worked with thousands of adolescents and parents. What has emerged is a clear understanding of two distinct and opposing worlds, the world of teenagers (*Teen World*) and the world of parents (*Grownup World*). These worlds have divergent realities and tremendous difficulty co-existing in a single universe. Ten Tips represents an effort to help these two worlds live and work with each other peacefully.

Ten Tips is not a panacea for the plethora of problems that parents ponder today. However, Ten Tips i_s an easy to understand and entertaining guide for you and your teenagers. Ten Tips helps you to be more effective and connected with your kids. I guarantee this! By using the Ten Tips consistently, you decrease or maybe even eliminate power struggles with your teen. Imagine that! You're communication improves and more trust develops among all family members. Your sons or daughters learn how take on appropriate and necessary levels of responsibility. They learn how to make good decisions when faced with a problem or difficult situation. They hold themselves and others accountable for their commitments (including you). They become resourceful, resilient, competent and capable young adults.

Integrate the Ten Tips into the fabric of your family and you will have more fun with your teenager and they will be more open and cooperative. They will not need to be reminded to take out the trash or feed the dog. They will be doing those things on their own. Their room will become habitable again because they have decided they can't live like that anymore. They will show up when they say they will and so on. All of this and more happens when you use the Ten Tips every chance you get. Don't miss any opportunity to improve your relationship with your teen. Simply put, the Ten Tips, helps you and your teen do what it takes to succeed.

You may have read dozens of parenting books over the years but *Ten Tips to Tame Your Teen* is one of the only books to focus on relationships versus problems. If this book helps you to repair a broken relationship or simply helps you to be more patience and a better listener, then my efforts will have not been in vain.

Thank you for reading this book. Now put it to good use.

Sincerely,

Ray

Please visit my website, www.rayerickson.com or e-mail me at ray@rayerickson.com.

INDEX

Made in the USA
Charleston, SC
31 December 2013